Mrs. Edward Ashley Walker

**From the Crib to the Cross**

A Life of Christ in Words of One Syllabe

Mrs. Edward Ashley Walker

**From the Crib to the Cross**
*A Life of Christ in Words of One Syllabe*

ISBN/EAN: 9783337255046

Printed in Europe, USA, Canada, Australia, Japan

Cover: Foto ©Lupo / pixelio.de

More available books at **www.hansebooks.com**

# THE CRIB TO THE CROSS.

## A Life of Christ

### In Words of One Syllable,

Entered according to Act of Congress in the year 1869,
By Geo. A. Leavitt,
In the Clerk's Office of the District Court of the United States for the Southern District of New York.

I WANT to tell you all I can of the Life of Jesus Christ.

No one can write so good a life of Him as that which we have in God's own Word.

There, Matthew, Mark, Luke and John, have set down just what they, or some near friend of theirs, saw Christ do and heard Him say.

But men, from that time to this, have tried to find out all they could of His life, and of the land in which He dwelt.

You will like, some day, to read the books in which they tell these things. But just now you can not spell long words, so I thought I would try to write out a life of Christ for you in such short words that you could read it with your own eyes.

It is more years than most of you can count since Christ was born, and He was still a young man when He died, and the land which was His home is far off from ours. Yet in spite of all this, His life has more to do with your life and mine to-day, than that of all our friends, the most near and dear.

One thing more I want to say to you. Jesus Christ, though He was the Son of God, was the Son of man as well. He was once a flesh and blood boy, just like the boys who read this, and the same world in which we now live was His home.

It may be you had no doubt of this, but I once knew a bright boy who had. He said one day, " You don't mean that Christ was in *my* world when they did those things to Him! Why, I thought all that was done up in the sky!"

No, it was not done up in the sky, but in

this world of ours, and the love and hate which were drawn forth by Christ's words and deeds, came out of just such hearts as ours.

Your grown up friends will know that I can not write a book in short words such as this is is to be, and not at times change the form of Christ's words more than I could wish. But I trust, with all my heart, that I may not lead you to false views of what He taught and what He did, and that this book will, at least, lift you up where you can catch one glimpse of Him, whom to know as He is, will be the task and the joy of all good hearts from age to age.

# PREFATORY NOTE.

PROPER names are, of course, unchanged in this book; no other words of more than one syllable have been used, except "baptize" (once), and "Father" and "Holy Ghost" (twice). These variations from the monosyllabic rule seemed unavoidable.

FROM

# THE CRIB TO THE CROSS:

A LIFE OF CHRIST.

ONCE there was a young girl whose name was Mary. Her home was in a small town on the white hills of Galilee.

Mary was poor, and not much known in the world, but God knew her, and chose her out of all that world to give birth to His Son.

One day Gabriel flew down from God to Nazareth, where her home was, to bring Mary this good news. He told her, too, just when the child would be born, and what name she must give him.

Mary's heart must have been full of strange thoughts, but all she said was, "I am the Lord's maid; let it be with me as He shall please."

Then Gabriel flew back to God with this sweet, meek word from Mary, and no one in all the world knew that he had been here.

There was no one in Nazareth to whom Mary could tell the glad news, but she went at once to see a near friend of hers, who was the wife of a priest far off in Hebron. She must have been four or five days on the way, but at the end of her long ride Mary found she had no need to tell the good news. As soon as Elizabeth (that was her friend's name) saw her come in at the door, she cried out with joy, and said, "What am I, that she who is to give birth to my Lord, should come to me!"

When she heard these words, Mary sang a grand hymn of praise, and her song is still sung in the Church, and you may have heard it there.

Mary staid with her friend three months, and then went back to Nazareth. She had not been gone long when Elizabeth's son John was born. We shall hear more of him by and by, and what he thought of Mary's son when they both grew to be men.

There was a good man in Nazareth, whose name was Joseph, and Mary had said that she would be his wife. Joseph had a dream one night, in which God told him all that had been said to Mary, and bade him take her home to live with him, and when her child should be born, call his name Jesus. In the Jews' tongue, Jesus means one who saves. So Joseph did as God bade him.

Now it came to pass in those days, that a law was made that all the Jews should have their names put down on the roll which was to be sent to Rome for great Cæsar, the king of all the world, to see.

The Jews were not free then, but the slaves of Rome.

Joseph had to go a long way to give in his name. He went to his own town, which was four score miles from Nazareth.

He was poor, like Mary, but he was of high birth. In fact, he may have been the true heir to the throne, for he was of King David's race, and

Bethlehem was David's home, you know. So to Bethlehem Joseph went, and as Mary seems to have had no friends but this brave, kind man, she did not like to be left at home, but took the long ride with him.

There was such a great crowd in the small town of Bethlehem, that by the time Joseph and Mary got there the inn was full. They were glad to lay their heads in the place where the beasts were kept. It was in what we should call the barn of the inn, that they found rest. It may be that this barn was a cave in the rocks. Men in that land like to save work, and so they are quite apt to take a cave for one room, and build their house in front of it. They do not keep their beasts so far from them as we do.

In this cave, or shed, the Christ child was born that night. In the East, they do not dress a babe in long robes, but take long bands of cloth, half a foot wide, and wind them round and round him from his neck to his feet. Mary put such bands as these on her child, and laid him in his crib. Do you know what sort of a crib he had? It was just the rock, or stone trough out of which the beasts ate! Joseph and Mary made it as soft as they could with hay and straw, but at the best, what a bed it was to lay such a child in! I must now tell you who first came to see Jesus, and how they knew that such a child had been born.

In that land great flocks of sheep were kept at that time. They did not fence their fields as we do, so that men had to watch their flocks all night, that no sheep might stray off, nor be caught by wild beasts which came out at night to prowl for food.

It was in these fields of Bethlehem that young David took care of his sheep. Here it was that he did that brave deed of which he told King Saul. Here he slew two wild beasts, the king of beasts and a bear.

"He came and took a lamb out of the flock," said he, "and I went out and smote him to save it out of his mouth. I caught him by his beard, and smote him and slew him."

He slew both these beasts when he was a boy in these fields. But long, long years have gone by, and in those fields men still watch their flocks.

Who they were we do not know,

but all at once they saw a grand sight, such as all the kings on earth would have been proud to have seen, if God had let them. But God is apt to show His best things to a child, or to those souls that are most like a child. He gave these men who kept their sheep on the hills, a glimpse of His own bright hosts on their march through the sky, and let them hear a song from His own choir!

Though the birth of Jesus made no stir at all on this poor earth which He came to bless, yet all the great world on high was full of light, and joy, and song, in praise of the new born king. When this light from on high first shone on the men, they were full of fear, it was so bright and strange. But a voice soon said to them, " Fear not! I bring you good news of great joy, which shall be to all the world. To you is born this day, in David's town, Jesus, which is Christ the Lord!"

Then when they had been told where this child could be found, they saw all at once that the sky was full of the hosts of God, and they heard them sing:

> "Praise to God the Most High!
> On earth peace, good will to men!"

But this bright scene soon went by, and the men were left with their sheep, to think of all that they had seen and heard.

They did not think long, but soon rose, and said, "Let us now go to Bethlehem and see the thing which has come to pass which the Lord hath made known to us."

Now they knew that God's own Son had come down to the earth to seek and save His lost sheep (that is what God's book calls us all), they did not care so much for their flocks. They left them there on the hills with the stars to watch them, and went straight to that crib in Bethlehem. There they found all things as they had been told they should. The babe, and Mary, and Joseph, the men from the fields and the beasts of the stall!

Men have tried and tried to paint that group from that age to this, but though they do their best, they can not show us just how grand it must have been. In the sketch which I like best, there is no light at all in the rough cave, but that which shines in the eyes of the Christ child. But this light is so strong, that the men who have just come in from the fields can not bear its blaze, but shield their eyes from it. This light streams forth from the child's face and makes the poor hut more bright than a king's house. Its rays touch here the bare stone walls and the rough straw and hay, and change them to gold, and there the pure brow of Mary, the forms of the men from the fields who lean on their crooks, and the ox who looks down with mild eyes on the strange guest in his crib.

It is not strange that these men, when they went out from such a scene as this, should have told all whom they met what they had seen in the sky and seen in the cave. But we do not hear that the news made the least stir in the town.

When the child Jesus was not quite six weeks old he went to Jerusalem.

It was a law with the Jews that each boy that was born should go to the Lord's House at that age.

The rich took a lamb with them and gave it to the priest. Mary and Joseph were too poor to own a lamb, so they took two doves for their gift.

When Joseph and Mary came in to the house of the Lord, they found there an old man whose name was Simeon. He had been told that he should not die till he had seen "the Lord's Christ." God had led him there that day to meet this child from Bethlehem, and he knew at once when he saw him that this was the Lord's

Christ. How must Mary have felt when this wise old man, whom all knew to be one who could see things which were yet to come, took her babe in his arms and broke out in a grand song of praise to God! His next act was to bless Joseph and Mary. To Mary he spoke some strange, sweet words, for her to think of all her life. But he told her, too, that grief as well as joy, should come to her through this child; "A sword shall pierce through thy own soul!" She felt that sword when that dear head, which now lay on old Simeon's breast, was made to wear the crown of thorns but a few years from that time. But when Simeon had said these words, there came in one who, like him, was well known in all Jerusalem. Her name was

Anna, and she, too, saw the child, and gave thanks to God, and told the glad news of his birth to all whom she knew had hope that He who was to save them would soon come. Then the three went back to Bethlehem, where they soon had strange guests.

When Christ was born in Bethlehem, the sky told the glad news to more than those Jews who kept watch of their flocks near the inn.

Far off, in a strange land, there were wise men who knew much of the worlds which fill the sky with their light, and read the stars as if they had been books.

They had read, too, in an old scroll, that a wise man of an age long past had said that A STAR should come out of Jacob, and bring great things to those on whom it should shine. So their eyes swept the skies each night in the hope they could catch sight of this Star, whose time they were sure must be near at hand. And one night it came! There it was, new and bright, as it had just come from God's hand to point with its rays straight to the far off place where the Christ child lay. Then they were sure that the King of the Jews must have come, and were full of joy, and made haste to get choice gifts and go and lay them at His feet. The gifts they took with them were such as men give to kings ; they were gold, and myrrh, and rare drugs.

On they came with their train of men and beasts, all the way from Persia or Arabia to Jerusalem. When at last they came to the great town, they thought they should find it full of joy that the Christ had come. But they could find no one there who knew that such a child had been born!

How strange it must have been to the wise men to see these Jews rush to and fro through the streets, full of their small cares and joys, but with no thought of Him whom God had sent to save them!

But it was not small faith which had brought these men so far, and so they did not give up their search when they found that the rest of the world had no thought or care that the true King of the Jews had come. They made such a stir in the town, as they went here and there to ask the same thing, "Where is He that is born King of the Jews, for we have seen His star in the East, and have come to bow down to Him," that the news found its way to the king on the throne.

Now at last the wise men had found some one who had an ear for their strange tale. But Herod was not glad when he heard it, but full of fear. False Jew and vain man that he was, he did not like to hear of a new born king, for he thought he should have to give up his throne. Christ did not want that poor mean throne of Herod with all its blood stains; He came to reign in the heart of each child of man in all the wide world, and His reign was to have no end. But Herod was too bad and dull to take in such a grand plan as this; so he made a vile plan of his own.

He sent in haste to call all the chief priests and scribes to meet, and search the old books, and tell him where the Christ should be born. From the time of the first man till now, the world had known that Christ would come at some time, but Herod was not sure where he would choose his birth place. He did not have to wait long. The chief priests and scribes told him that Christ was to be born in Bethlehem. "Out of Bethlehem shall come He who shall rule Israel!"

The words were as plain as could be, and did not put the old king's fears to rest at all.

He next sent, by stealth, for the wise men from the East, that he might find out just when they had seen the Star. Then he made a great show of zeal that Christ should be found. He bade them go to Bethlehem, five or six miles from town, and search for "the young child, and when ye have found him, bring me word, that I, too, may come and bow down to him!"

The wise men were not so wise that they could read the hearts of men, so they thought Herod spoke the truth. They went out from the false king with glad hearts, and made their way to Bethlehem.

I have heard an old tale, which may or may not be true. Here it is:

The wise men, with their train of slaves and beasts, cross the plain and climb the hills till they reach the gate of Bethlehem. While they are in doubt which way to turn next, they halt by a well to rest. As they stoop to draw from the well, a flash of light comes from its depths! They look up with joy, and see just in front of them that same bright Star which they had seen in their far off home at the East!

As I said, this may not be true, but there is a well there at the gate, and I can tell you a true tale of it.

When David was a man of war, the great host of his foes were once in Bethlehem, and he and his men of war were hid in the rocks near the town. David must have been home sick, I think, for all at once he cried out, "O that one would give me drink from the well of Bethlehem which is by the gate!" His three chief braves heard of this wish of David, and at the risk of their life broke through the host of their foes to the well, and then made their way back to the rocks with their prize! But David would not drink it, when they brought him the draught. He said it cost too much for him to drink, so he gave it to the Lord.

It is quite true, too, that the wise men had to pass by this well, and that they saw the Star once more as they had seen it in the East. Matthew speaks of the great joy with which they saw it, and tells us how it led them on till at last it stood still, and sent its rays down on the place where Jesus, and Mary, and Joseph had their home. They had found what they had sought through long days of toil and care. Who can guess how glad they were?

They made their way in where the

young child was, and fell at his feet. When they had done this, their slaves brought in the rich store of gifts and they laid all at the babe's feet where they had just knelt.

The love which had brought them so far to see him, must have been worth more to Christ than the best gifts they had brought.

The home He had just left is more grand than tongue can tell. The gates are pearls, and the streets gold, and the air is full of sweet sounds and scents, such as are not known by name on earth. But Jesus knew that this red gold and the sweets of Arabia, which the wise men gave Him, meant love and praise. So we may be sure that His smiles made them glad they had sought Him out, and brought their best to Him. The last we hear of them is, that God sent them a dream to warn them how false King Herod was. So they went home by a new way.

Do you not think that the thought of the dear face of the child, as His eyes fell on them and their gifts, must have made their way home more bright than the star had made their road to Bethlehem?

But Jesus had now a long ride to take. When the wise men were gone, Joseph, too, had a dream. In it God spoke to him, and bade him take Jesus and Mary, and flee to the land of Egypt, and stay there till he should be told it was safe to bring them back. He told him, too, that this child who had such strange guests, and of whom such grand things had been said as he lay in old Simeon's arms, had a strong foe. Jesus had been heard of in the king's house, and the bad old man, whose hands were red with blood, meant to get this heir to the throne of David out of the way.

When Herod found that it was of no use to watch the road from Bethlehem more, for the wise men had gone home, and left him in the dark as to what they had seen there, he was mad with fear and rage.

There was no star to point out to him the house in which Jesus was, but do you know what he did to make sure that the young king should be put to death? He had all the boys in Bethlehem, who were not yet two years old, slain! It has been said that Herod was such a fiend in his fear lest the new born King should rob him of his throne, that he had his own boy put to death, too, lest he might prove to be the Christ!

But through Joseph's care, Mary and her child were safe in Egypt while so much blood was shed in Bethlehem. They had to flee by night, lest Herod's men of war should track them, and kill the Prince of Life.

They had to stay in that strange land for some months, so the gold which the wise men had left with them must have been of great use to them.

But King Herod died at last, and left his throne to his three sons.

Once more God spoke to Joseph in a dream, and said, " Rise, and take the young child and Mary and go to the land of Israel, for they are dead who sought the young child's life."

So back they went to their own land. But the first thing which Joseph heard when they got there, was such bad news, that he felt it would not be safe to take the child to Bethlehem. Herod was dead to be sure, but one of his sons now had rule in that part of the land, and the first act of this son's reign had been to kill a vast crowd of men who did not please him. So Joseph took Jesus to the north, to that town on the hills where Mary and he had their first home.

Just one short verse tells us all we can know of the next ten years of Christ's life. We learn from it that He grew in size; that he grew more and more wise; and that the grace of

God was on Him. I have read in old books some things which men have thought Jesus must have done when he was a child. But some of these things are so false to all that we know of the meek, pure Jesus, that we can not trust those which seem as if they might have been true.

We know that Nazareth was not a large town, and that all who dwelt there must have seen this boy as he went up and down the steep streets, or was at work with Joseph in his shop, or went with Mary to the well. He must have had strange thoughts in his mind of what was to come to him and be done by him in the years; and those who went to school with him, or could play with him from time to time, must have found him a brave, true, sweet mate ; but we do not learn from God's word that he was thought of as not just like all the rest of the boys of the town.

The next time we hear of Christ is in God's own Book, he is twelve years old, and has gone to Jerusalem, which is three score and ten miles from his home—a score is twice ten, you know. Spring had come, and with it the great Feast of the year.

To all boys who were born Jews it must have been a grand thing to come of age, so that they, too, could go to the Feast and take their place with the men. It was the law that they should do this when they were twelve years old.

You know there were no cars in those days. Not a coach, or a chaise, or a cart, or the least thing to ride in was known on those hills. There was not a road in all the land like ours. At the best, these were mere paths where the mule, with its sure foot, could tread, and the men and boys pick their way.

Then there were swarms of thieves, who hid in the rocks, to pounce on all who went by, if they were so few that it was safe to rob them.

So when the time drew near to go to the Feast, the Jews would make up large trains of friends and town's men, so that all might be safe.

You can see that the mere trip to Jerusalem must have been a great treat to a boy, not at all like our hum drum rides in the cars. There would be the ride on the mule, part of the way, in the Spring, when all things were fresh, and green, and in sweet bloom. There would be the brisk run on the smooth plain with play mates from home, or friends who dwelt so far off that this would be the one time in the year to meet them. There would be the climb up the steep rocks, with the chance, at each turn, that a band of thieves might spring out on the train and rob them, or put them to rout. A bold, brave boy, might have half a hope and half a fear that he might see such a sight.

Then at night there would be the camp by the side of the road, or in the yard of some lone inn. The boys would help lift the loads from the backs of the mules, and make the beasts fast to stakes, so they could not stray. The bright fires would soon blaze on all sides, at which to cook the food they had brought from home. When the meal was done, there would be the gay chat and songs of the groups here and there.

Then when all were laid down to rest, a strange hush would come on all things, the camp fires would die out, and the stars shine out one by one. Then the boy would lie and gaze at the bright roof of his strange bed room, with its blue and gold, and now and then a soft white cloud to veil it, till his eyes would close in sleep.

At dawn the din of the crowd would wake him, as they broke camp, and made haste to set out on their way ere the hot sun rose. Then as they went on, the train would chant some grand old psalm like that which says :

"I was glad when they said to me,
Let us go to the House of the Lord!"

At last the great town would come in view, and what a sight it must have been to a boy who had heard of what God had done for his race, and how rich and grand this chief town had been made! All boys in that land would hear this tale as soon as they could speak. They did not have piles of books as you do, but got all their tales from the lips of their friends and the wise men who sat at the gates. There was but one theme to all these tales, and that was what a grand race were the Jews; how brave in time of war, how rich in time of peace, and how dear to the heart of God!

But the chief sight of all the town was the House of God. It was built on a high hill. The whole great pile was half a mile square. Think of a church as large as that! Six or eight times the size of your church and mine. It was built of pure white stone. Round it was a wall one score and five feet high; a long flight of steps led up to it; and there were nine great gates by which you could pass in. These gates were more than two score feet high, and half as wide, and shone with white and gold.

Then as the train wound in through the gates of the town, what joy there must have been to a boy from the hills, in all the strange, new sights of the streets. The streets were not wide, and the throng would be so great, it would be hard to get through, but that would give all the more zest. Such crowds went to Jerusalem at the time of this Feast, that the town could not hold them, though each man who dwelt there made his house free to those who came.

Not a few of the trains would have to camp out on the hills, as near the gate as they could find room.

As soon as the train had found a place to camp, all things would be put in trim for a week's stay, and rooms found where they could keep the great Feast. The law was, that not a bit of the lamb (which made the chief part of the feast) should be left. In the case of a small house like Joseph's, a lamb would be quite too much for one meal, so the law bade ten or more friends club for the Feast. They would choose one to be at the head and to take care that all things were done as they should be. This chief, as we will call him, had to take the live lamb on his back, and go up to the House of God with it. This must be done just at sun set.

When the chief had slain the lamb, it had to pass through the hands of three priests, who kept the fat and the blood.

Then the chief took it back to his club, and it was put on spits, in the form of a cross, to roast, and the law was most strict that they should not break a bone of it.

That night, as soon as the lamb

was done, they all sat down to the great Feast of the week.

First the chief said grace, and a course of herbs, etc., came on. Next the lamb was brought in, and at this point, the boys who came to the Feast had a part to play, more· than to help make way with the food.

They were to turn to the chief of the Feast, and say, " What mean these things, sir ? Why do we eat these dry, thin cakes, and these herbs of Egypt? Why must the lamb be slain in God's own House, and with such care that not a bone should break ?"

Then the chief would tell the old tale of the dark days of their race. How Jacob and his sons had been near death in their own land for want of food, when God made their crops fail. How they had gone down to Egypt to buy corn, and found their own Joseph there, whom they had sold to be a slave, but who had now come to be a great man, next to the king in might. How they had all made that land their home.

But by and by, when long years had past, a new king had come to the throne, who had not known Joseph at all, and did not care for what he had done for Egypt. This king did not like these Jews who grew strong and rich so fast. He had his fears that they would soon own all the land, and drive out the old race who dwelt there. So he made haste and bound them as slaves. They had to work hard, and bear great wrongs for long years, till God sent Moses to help them.

Then the chief would tell the boys of the ten plagues which God sent on the king and all his land, to make him let go his hold on the Jews. You know what these plagues were, and the last of them was the cause of that Feast which they were now met to keep.

In one night the first born son in each house was put to death. The Jews were not hurt by this plague. God bade each house of all their tribes take a lamb, kill it at sun set, roast it, and eat it that same night. But they were first to take some of its blood, and mark the posts of their doors, so that when Death should go up and down the streets to slay God's foes, he should know that where those blood stains were on the doors, there dwelt those who were the friends of God, and spare them.

That night there was a great cry in Egypt, for there was not a house (save the homes of the Jews) where there was not one dead.

But the Jews were then set free, and led forth by Moses to the good land, and had kept this Feast from year to year, as God bade them, from that time to this.

And then the chief might tell the boys that though they were now once more in bonds to a strange race, yet the Christ of God would one day come and break the yoke off their necks, and sit on the throne of David; and that it might be that some who sat there would live to see his face in the flesh!

We should all like to know if at this Feast in the spring of A.D. 8 (A.D. stands for "the year of our Lord"), it fell to the lot of Jesus to ask the chief of their club, "What mean these things, sir?"

How much more that boy could have told those who sat there, than the chief could tell him! How much more of what God had done in times past for the Jews, and most of all, of what He meant to do for the Jews and all the world, by means of His Son who sat with them there! What a thrill it would have sent through them all if the King who was to set them free, and who sat there a child in the midst of them, had said, "I who speak to you am He!"

But it seems that the Feast went

by with no such words from the Boy of Nazareth. His time had not yet come.

The week of good cheer, and song, and joy, came to an end, and then the train set out for home.

Mary and Joseph did not see Jesus as they went out through the gate of the town. But this did not vex them in the least. He was not a boy whom they had to watch lest he should go wrong. They could trust him out of their sight. He had won the love of all who knew him, and they thought he had gone on with some of his mates or their kin.

So they had no thought of care till they had got to the end of the first day's stage. It was night now, and Mary's heart could not rest till she had seen with her own eyes that her boy was well fed; and had a nice place to sleep. So she and Joseph sought him on all sides. But he was to be found with none of the groups, and no one had the least news to tell of him.

It was plain that Jesus had not left town at all, so back they had to go in search of him.

How they came to look for him in God's House at last, is more than we know, but there they found him on the third day from the close of the feast. He was in one of the courts where the wise men of the Jews were wont to meet to talk of the deep things of their law. The pair who have sought him so long, see a group of the great men of Jerusalem, here a judge, there a priest, and there a scribe, with long gray beards and grave brows, and keen eyes all bent on the bright young face of their lost child! There he sits, not bold and rude, but with all the ease of a dear child in his own home, and hears what these wise men have to say, and speaks such words to them as stir their minds to the depths.

Who shall say that Mary did not, at that hour, feel the first prick of the sword which old Simeon had told her should one day pierce through her own heart? There sits her child, and yet not her child. There is a far off look in his eyes, and strange words are on his lips. Can it be that the still life of that home at Nazareth, so dear to Mary, and so dear to him till now, is at an end?

Half wild with grief, and worn out

by long search for him, Mary breaks in on the hush of that awe struck group with a cry wrung from her heart of hearts, "Son! why hast thou dealt thus with us! Lo, we have sought thee with sad hearts."

To this the child said, "How is it that you sought me? Did you not know that I must do my FATHER's work (or be in my FATHER's House)?"

As if he had said, "Where should the son of God be at home but in God's own House?"

But his time had not yet come, so he rose and left the group of wise men and went out with Joseph and Mary, and back to Nazareth.

There he dwelt with them for years. The Jews taught all their boys, rich or poor, a trade. Jesus learnt his trade at Joseph's bench, where he made ploughs and yokes of wood.

I read not long since of a poor lame dwarf, whose trade it was to make toys. He said to a friend who came to see him at his work, that though God's word did not tell us so, yet it did him good to think that Jesus' love for the young was shown in the same way with his own. That Jesus as he stood at the bench at work, or to watch Joseph's work, was sure to save all the chips and make toys out of them for some poor child, who would have had no toy but for him, and who stood at the door to wait for it with shy glad eyes! I like to think so, too, and it is far more like what we know of Jesus, the man, than most of the made up tales which are told of Jesus, the child, in the old books. We may be sure that he who took such pains to clasp the dear babes in his arms when he was a man, worn out with toil, had not let slip in all his life the least chance to be kind to them. So, though God does not choose to tell us much of those years of Christ's youth, yet we are sure to be right if we think of him as rich in kind deeds and words to all who came near him, through them all.

But now we come to the true tale of the last three years of Christ's life.

There was a man near of kin to Jesus, whose name was John. He was the son of that Elizabeth whom, as I told you, Mary went to see as soon as Gabriel, who brought her the good news, had left her.

We know still less of John's youth than of that of Jesus.

All that is said of him in God's Word is, that he grew, and grew strong of soul, and did not live in the town, but out in the free wilds, till the day when he made known that he was sent by God to clear a path for the feet of His Son Jesus. But now it is A.D. 26, and John is one score and ten years old, and the news spreads more and more that he is a great man. Crowds go out to find him, and see what new thing he will say to them.

They find a rough, strong man with long hair and beard, which have not been cut in all his life. His dress is a long robe of cloth, which was made out of hair, not soft like lamb's wool, but harsh and coarse, and tied at the waist by a strip of skin. His food is what the wilds can give him. It is the sweet comb which the bees hide for him in clefts of the rocks and holes in the trees, and a sort of bug which men still eat, at times, in that land. When he stands up to preach with his strange dress, and his long locks which float in the wind, and his sharp, stern words, all quail. He had no soft words for rich or poor. He brought the sin of each home to all who heard him, and bade each turn at once, and do right where he had done wrong. He put his hand right on the sin that was most dear to them.

But there was a wild sort of charm in his looks and bold speech, so that a great crowd, when they had heard him, went to him to have him baptize

PREACHING OF JOHN THE BAPTIST.

them at the Jordan, near which he now stood. He made use of this rite as a sign that those who came to him for it must have a change of heart and life. Not a few who heard him thought he must be the Christ. But he would not let them think this of him at all. He said, " I am not the Christ, but am sent first to clear the way for the Christ. I am not fit to loose Christ's shoe from his foot."

One day, as he stood at the ford of Jordan, a young man came with the crowd to hear him preach. His dress was like that of the rest of the young men, and he made no more claim than the rest. But John saw him at once, and knew him to be he of whom he spake.

He was of his kin to be sure, but

Christ's home had been in the town all these years, and John's had been in the wilds, and though they may have met at some of the feasts in Jerusalem, yet their homes were not near.

But John had heard, when a young child, the strange tale of Gabriel's words to Mary; of Elizabeth's faith that Mary's son was her Lord and the world's Lord; and of the men who left their sheep to go and bow down in the cave at the babe's feet, and the wise men, who came next; and of old Simeon's cry of joy as he held the babe in his arms, and Anna's good news, which she told all whose hopes were set on the Christ.

John had known that Christ would be made known some day. That he was hid through such long years would not shake John's faith in the least. They did not live so fast then as we do. Boys did not rush from the boy's life to the man's life, in such mad haste as now. The Jews would not have thought a man whose years were less than one score and ten, fit at all to preach, or do a great work in the world.

But John, as well as Jesus, when once he set out on his life's work, did it with all his might. John's time of work was but for a few months, but how much he did! And Christ's great work, which was to save a world, was all done in three short years!

But as I said, John saw Christ, and knew that his time was come. He was so sure of this, that when Christ came to him for the same rite which the throng take from his hands, he drew back.

"No," he said; "who am I that I should do such a thing? I have need to take this rite from thee."

But Christ bids him do what he asks at his hands, and John minds him at once. Now, once more the world on high, as at Christ's birth, takes heed of what is done on earth. As Jesus comes up out of Jordan, the veil is drawn back which hides that bright world, and a pure white dove floats down and rests on his head, while a voice, which all knew must be that of God, breaks in on the still scene, and says: "This is my dear Son!"

Next came a scene far more strange than that we have just left on the banks of the Jordan. I shall not, of course, try to tell you all that it meant. You and I will both know more of what Christ went through in the next month's time, by and by. The best I can do is to tell you, in a few words, what I think it meant.

God's word says that Christ went right to the wilds when he left John. There he staid for two score days and two score nights, with the wild beasts, as Mark says, and with no food.

At first his mind must have been so full of plans for his great task, and with thoughts of all that he must do and bear, and all the pain he must bring to the hearts of those to whom he was dear, that he would not feel the want of food. But at last this weak flesh of ours, which he wore as well as you and I, with just the same wants which you and I feel each hour of our lives, grew faint, and cried out for food. At this point Satan, who has been on the watch all the time, thinks his chance has come, so he creeps up to the faint, worn man who lies there on the bare rocks, which yield not so much as a place for the bees to hide their sweets.

"If you are the Son of God, as you have thought you were all the days you have been out here, just turn some of these stones to bread."

Jesus is not so weak that he does not know at once who it is who speaks. In "The Pilgrim's Progress," you know, poor Christian goes through the Shadow of Death, and if you will read the sad tale of all he had to meet there, it may help you to guess at a small part of what Christ bore at this time. But when the fiends crept up to Christian to hiss bad things in his ear, the poor man did not know who spoke to him. He thought the bad things came out of his own heart, and this made them ten times more hard to bear.

But Jesus had not one sin in his heart, so he knew that the voice could not come from there; and it could not come from God, for God had not sent his Son down to this world to make bread, or use his might at all for his own wants. So Christ turns at once on Satan with a sharp dart out of God's Word. Man is more than flesh, and so mere bread will not give him the strength he wants. He is a soul, and must be fed by all God's words, or he will starve. We hear no more as to Christ's want of food. Satan's thrust seems to rouse him to full life and strength, of flesh as well as soul. But Satan tries once more.

"If you will not use your might to feed your own weak flesh, use it to make the world stare, and show them at once how great you are. Go back to Jerusalem, and jump from the top of that spire of God's house which is most high in the air. Jump right down in the midst of the great crowd which throng the courts, and as they see you still live, they will know you are God's own Son; as all your plan to preach, and work cures from town to town, will not make them know it."

And this time Satan thought he

would quote God's word first, so he adds, " You know it is said He shall give His hosts charge to keep thee, and in their hands they shall bear thee up, lest thou dash thy foot on a stone!"

" It is said, ' Thou shalt not tempt the Lord thy God!' " is all which Christ said, or had need to say, to turn this thrust. Then. Satan drew back, that he might bring all his force to bear on one last charge. He spreads out to Christ's view the whole world. Then he speaks words which seem to mean this : You see in what a state all things are. Your own dear race are slaves now, but if you will bow down to me, and own that my rule is best ; take me for your guide, and use the same means with men that I do, you can raise your race and sit on the throne of the world, and draw all men to you. My way will give you a crown soon, and all the world at your feet; your way will give you two or three years of toil and pain, and a cross and a tomb at the end.

"Get thee hence, Satan!" cries Jesus, and Satan flies, to tempt him no more, and the hosts of God come to soothe and feed him who has borne so much.

It was not quite six weeks from the day when Jesus had met John at the Jordan for the first time, that he went to him once more. As John saw him come, he cried to the throng who were with him, "This is the Lamb of God, who bears the sins of the world!"

Till this time John seems to have said sharp, strong things of the sins of all who heard him, and bade them get rid of their sins at once. But now he sees in Christ, and bids all see in him, the one way by which a soul can be freed from its sins—" the Lamb of God, who bears the sins of the world!"

John the Baptist was at the head of a sort of school. Not a few who came to hear him preach, would stop to be taught by him more and more, and spend all their time with him. The next day, as John stood with two of these friends with him, he spied Jesus as he went by, and said once more, " This is the Lamb of God!"

At this, these friends, whose names were John and Andrew, leave the side of John Baptist, and push on till they come so near Jesus that he hears their steps. He turns and looks at them, and says, "What seek ye?"

"Lord, where dost thou dwell?"

"Come and see."

So they go, and spend the night with him. Andrew was the son of Jonas; and Jonas had one more son, of whom we shall hear much in times to come. His name was Simon Peter, and as soon as Andrew has found out where Christ dwells, he goes and finds Peter, and tells him the glad news, "We have found the Christ!" and brings him to the place where they are to lodge with Jesus that night. The next day Jesus and the three friends set out for a long walk, no less than three score miles long. On the way, Christ finds a new friend, whose name is Philip, and bids him go with him.

He minds at once, and he learns so much of Jesus as he walks and talks with him on the way, that he, too, like Andrew, thinks of a dear friend whom he longs to bring to know and love him too, as the Christ of God.

So as soon as they get to Cana, Philip goes in search of his old friend Nathanael, and tells him that he has found him who has been the theme of their talks and their hopes for so long a time. But when Nathanael hears that their new lord is a Nazareth man, he has not much faith in him.

Nazareth has a bad name far and near, and Nathanael can't think that the true Christ would choose such a vile town for his home. But to please his friend he goes with him to take a look at his new Lord. Christ sees the doubts in his heart as he comes near, and sweeps them all out with a few words. He proves that though he is Jesus of Nazareth, the son of Joseph, yet he is the Son of God as well. There is a fig tree near Cana where Nathanael goes to pray; where he can see no one but God and his own heart, and no one but God can see him. But Jesus tells Nathanael that he had seen him as he knelt there in the shade of that fig tree. That he found him first, when Philip was still in search of him. He makes the proof so strong that Nathanael's faith leaps at once as high as Philip's, who has spent three or four days with Christ, and he cries out in his joy, " Thou art the Son of God! Thou art the King of Israel!"

So Christ has five friends with him now : the two sons of Jonas, Andrew and Peter ; John, the son of Zebedee ; Philip, who was from the same town with them, and Nathanael.

Bar, means son, and Nathanael was the son of Tholomai ; so we know him by the name of Bar-tholemew.

Peter, too, we hear of at times, by the name of Simon Bar-Jona, which means son of Jonas.

It seems as if Christ took this long walk up to Cana just to go to a bride's feast! We do not know who the pair were. Some have thought that the groom was Christ's new friend, John, but there is no proof of this.

Mary was at the feast, and seems to have had some charge of things which she would not have had as just one of the guests.  As the feast draws near to an end, the wine fails, and Mary goes at once to her Son in this strait. .She does not go to the chief of the feast who sits at the head of the board, and whose place it is to see that all things are done as they should be, but she goes to Jesus, who is a mere guest.  " They have no wine!" she says.  His words do not read to us as if there were much hope that he would help them in the case.

" What have I to do with thee? Mine hour is not yet come."

But they must have had a tone which gave Mary hope, for she at once bids those who stand by to wait on the guests, go to Christ for what they need.  When next they want wine, then, they go to Christ, and he points to the great jars which stand in the court yard, and bids them fill them to the brim. They do so, and then he bids them draw out from these full jars, and take what they draw to the chief of the feast, who has not as yet found out that there is a want of wine. The men know that what they pour in the jars came out of the well, but what must they have thought when they draw out of the same jars bright, red wine! They take it to the chief, and as soon as he tastes it, he calls the groom, and says, " The way is to give good wine in the first part of a feast, and worse at the end ; but you have kept the good wine till now!"

It looks as if Christ did this deed just to please Mary, and save his host from the blame of scant fare at his feast. But it must have made those five new friends of his feel that he was in truth the Son of God.

At the end of this feast, Jesus went with Mary and Andrew and Peter to Capernaum, and staid there till spring came, and it was time for the same great feast to which he went when he was twelve years old.

We have just seen Jesus a guest at a gay feast. He was there, and there to make the scene more bright and glad with his smiles. Now we shall see that he can frown as well.

As he goes up the long flight of steps to God's House in Jerusalem, he hears strange sounds from the court which runs round the whole of it. This court is a sort of hall, broad and high, but it is part of the church. Here the scribes taught the law. This was the place where the Gentiles could come; they could not go up the next flight of steps to the church; but here they might stay and get what good they could from this "court of the Lord's House." From this court Jesus does not hear the soft hum of those who pray, and those who teach, but rude sounds of trade, the cries of beasts, and the clink of coin.

As he goes in a strange scene meets his eye. The pure floor, wrought in choice stones, is strewn with filth and straw. Beasts of all the sorts which the Jews might use when they went to pay their vows to God in His house (the ox, the sheep, the dove), are tied to the grand shafts of rare stone on which the roof rests, and low, and boa, and coo, on all sides. Men sit at desks and change the coin of Rome for that of the Jews, or take the price of some beast just sold. What would you think of such sights and sounds in the porch and aisles of your church?

The Jews who came to this Feast from far off points, would wish to buy in Jerusalem their lamb or their doves; but God's house was not the place to buy and sell in.

Christ made a scourge of small cords, or of the reeds with which the floor was strewn, and drove them all out of the court and down the steps. Men and beasts all fled, not so much from fear of the small whip, as at the sight of Christ's stern face. He was Christ the King at that hour, and all quail at his frown. Then he pours out the coin and throws down the desks, and says to those who had doves for sale, "Take these things hence! make not my FATHER's House a place of trade!"

All must have seen in him one who had a right to rule in God's House.

The Jews ask him, to be sure, what sign he means to show next, now he has done such a bold act; but no one seems to have tried to make a stand, or to have found fault with him at all.

While Jesus is in Jerusalem at this time, he does show the crowds which flock to the feast not a few signs that prove to those who see them that he is sent from God, but we are not told what these signs were. But one thing we do know, these deeds brought him a new friend; a man of wealth and of high rank and a judge. His name was Nicodemus, and he came to see Jesus at night, for he had not yet so much faith that he would risk the scorn and wrath of his great friends, and go to see him in broad day light.

Jesus does not find fault with him for this, but he gives him a plain talk.

You must get some one to read you John iii., where you will find all which Jesus said to Nicodemus. Nicodemus went out from Christ's house that night a new man. He did not show the change at once, it may be, but he made it plain to all at last. Three years from this time, when it will be at far more risk that such a man can own Christ as his lord, Nicodemus will own him, as we shall see, in the broad light of day and at great cost.

Jesus next went out through the towns of Judea with his friends to teach. John Baptist is at Enon with his school, and he and Jesus seem to work on, side by side, for a time. But some of John's class are not much like John. They feel no joy, but spite, when they know how the crowds flock to hear Jesus, and try to stir up strife on this ground.

When they come to John with their tale, how grand he seems as he speaks to them: " Have I not told you all the time that I was not the Christ, but had come to make clear the path for Christ? I told you that he on whom the Dove should rest was the Christ; I have told you more than once that this man whom the throng seek, is the Lamb of God, who bears the sin of the world. He must wax, but I must wane. He that has faith in him shall have that life which shall not end, and he who has not faith in him shall not see life, but the wrath of God rests on him." There was not a mean spot in this great, brave, true heart of John. He saw those who had felt such pride in him and clung to him for months, all at once leave his school and join that of this new Lord, but no pang of hurt pride or grief seems to have found place in his good heart. His work was for God and not for his own fame, and if God's work was to be done by God's own Son, he was proud to be known as his friend, and full of joy in the work.

But Christ seems to have thought it best to leave Judea soon, and go back to his home up in Galilee. So he said good bye to John Baptist, whose face he was not to see more till they should meet, in three years time, on high.

As Christ and his friends are on their way, they reach, one day at noon, a place of which all Jews think a great deal. It is a well, said to have been dug by Jacob's own hands, near Sychar, the chief town of Samaria. Jesus was so tired by their long walk in the heat, that he sat down by the side of the well to rest, while his friends go through the gate of the town to buy food for them all.

While he sits there a Samaritan comes up to the well with her jar on her head, and Christ ask her to let him drink from it. She does not know what to make of this. She knows at once that he who speaks to her is a Jew, but why should he speak to her? The Jews so hate and scorn the Samaritans, that much as they love trade, they will not trade with them, much less will they ask the least gift at their hands, and speak of them as "dogs." But here sits a young Jew who asks her to do a kind deed for him!

This seems so strange to her that she begs him to tell her why he should do such a thing.

Jesus sits there to rest his worn out frame, but here is a dark soul sick with sin, which he can bless, so he tells her who he is and what he has come to do, not for the Jews, and for no one race, but for a world. He tells her that he can give her that which will quench her thirst so she shall thirst no more. She does not know that he means the thirst of the soul, but sees in a dim way that he who speaks such strange words can not be a mere man. He proves this to her by his next words, so she has no doubt of its truth. He shows her that he knows all her past life as well as her own heart knows it. Then she owns him as sent of God, and he talks with her some time of the great truths of God.

At last, when she has shown that she, too, though a Samaritan, looks for the Christ to come, and she says, "tell us all things," Jesus says, "I that speak to thee am he!" It is not strange that she should leave her jar at the well, and fly back to town, and say to all whom she met, "Come and see a man who told me all things that I have done in all my life! Is not this the Christ?"

When the friends of Jesus came back from town with the food they had bought, they beg him to eat.

They know how faint and worn he was when they left him, but they come back to find him full of life and zeal, as he talks with one whom they would not speak to. He talks to her, too, in quite as frank and free a way as he would to them of the deep things of God. When she has gone, and they beg him to eat, he says, "I have meat to eat that ye know not of," and as they are in doubt what these words can mean, he makes it plain to them that he speaks of meat for the best part of man, the soul, as he adds: "My meat is to do the will of Him who sent me, and bring His work in the world to an end." God's work in this world is to save men, and that is what Christ meant.

A crowd soon pour out through the gate of the town to see this strange Jew, who can read the heart and past life of one whom he meets for the first time.

Not a few who come to stare, stay to beg him to make his home with them, and say, this is in truth the Christ who shall save the world. But he could give but two days to them, and then he must push on up to Cana.

At Capernaum, which is so far from Cana that it takes six or eight hours to go there, dwelt a man of high rank in the court of the king. He had heard of that bride's feast some weeks since, when Christ had made wine flow in such a free way for the guests, and had heard, too, of the deeds he had wrought while in Jerusalem at the feast. His son lies at the point of death, and as soon as he hears that Jesus has come back to Cana, he starts at once to find him, and bring him back with him, that he may heal his son.

He has so much faith as to think that Christ can cure his son if he can get him to go to his house, but he learns that his might is more than the skill of a wise leech. The great man of Capernaum says to the poor man of Cana, " Sir, come down ere my child die!" But the poor man, who does not stir a step from the place where the great man found him, says, with the air of a king, "Go thy way; thy son lives." And he has a right to speak like a king, for he is the King of Life.

The great man seems to have had such sure faith in Christ's word, that he does not make haste home, for he is sure all is right there. We hear of him as on his way back the next day, when he meets some who have been sent to tell him the glad news that his son lives. When he asks at what hour the first signs of cure were seen, he finds that it was at the seventh hour (one o'clock); the same hour when he had been told by Christ that his son should live. So he and all his house have faith in Christ, and as

Christ soon went to Capernaum to live, we may guess that these good strong friends of his, whose son he had made well with a word, made him choose that place for his home. It was the place, too, where Andrew and Peter, and James, and John plied their trade, and Mary, when Joseph had died, went there to live, too.

Near this time Jesus went to his old home in Nazareth. He went to church, as it was his way to do. To this church Christ had been all the years of his boy life and youth. Here he had been to school, and as he went in on this day, he must have seen not a few who had been his friends in the old times.

But the fame of what he has done far off in the great town, and near by in Cana and Capernaum, has come to them in this small nest in the hills. The priest, when he sees him come in, hands him the scroll on which is that part of God's word which they had in those days. Christ stands up to read, and makes choice of part of Isaiah lxi., for his text. When he has read it, he shuts the book and sits down to preach, for that was the way in those days. All eyes are on him. What will he say first?

" This day what I have read to you has come to pass in me! I am he who was to come and preach to the poor, heal wounds of the heart, set the slaves free, give sight to the blind, and do good to all."

His words have a rare charm to all who hear ; but they can't get it out of their minds that Jesus was brought up in the midst of them. These are grand, sweet words, they say, but who is it who speaks them? No one but the son of Joseph; that boy whom we have seen at play and at work in our town, from year to year, for so long a time.

One might say, " Why I went to school with him ;" and one, " He did such and such a piece of work for us. How can he be what he claims to be? Why, we know him! but when the true Christ shall come, he will burst on the sight of all in the pomp and pride of a great king."

As he still speaks on, their doubt grows to be rage, and at last they mob him. They thrust him out of the church, and take him up to the cliff on which their town is built, and mean to cast him off, and make an end of him at once. But his hour to die had not yet come. He glides through the midst of the mean, fierce mob, and goes his way to bless towns which make no claim to know him as the son of Joseph, but are glad with all their hearts to know him as the Son of God.

He first goes back to Capernaum. This town lay on the Sea of Tiberias. That was not much of a sea as we should think, who have the two great seas and all the great lakes. This sea of Tiberias, or Galilee, was just a lake; not much more than twelve miles long and five or six miles wide.

But there was a great deal of trade

on it. There were six large towns on its shore. Here, too, were some springs, the fame of which brought crowds from far off towns and lands; and in one of its towns the king dwelt with his court a part of the year. So you see Christ could have found no one place in all the land from which he could reach such a host of souls as these shores of the sea of Galilee.

He had not been back from Nazareth long, when he went out for a walk on the shore. But those who have heard him in the church long to hear him more, and press out to find him. The crowd is so great that Christ looks for some place where he can stand to speak to them.

He spies two boats on the beach, while the men who own them are some way off at work on their nets, to cleanse them or mend them. He knows the men. They are his old friends, Andrew and Simon, and not far off are John and James, who are in trade with the sons of Jonas.

Christ calls Peter to come to him, and begs him to get in the boat with him, and let it drift out on the lake, so that he can speak to the throng from it. So Peter did so, and Jesus sat down and taught them.

When he had sent the crowd home, he bade Peter and his men push out on the lake and let down their nets for a draught. Peter said it would be of no use; they had been hard at work all the night long, and not caught a fish. But in spite of this he said, "At thy word I will let down the net."

The net fills at once with such a host of fish that it breaks with their weight, and they have to call Zebedee and his sons and their men to help draw them in, and they fill both boats with the fish! Peter is wild at their great haul, and he falls down at Jesus' knees and owns his sins as to God.

We do not know why these friends had not staid with Jesus all the time since the feast in Cana, but we do know that at this hour Andrew, and Peter, and James, and John, left fish and nets and boats, and went up and down the land with Jesus till he left the world. He told them that he would teach them how to catch men in place of fish.

On the next day of rest (which you know was the last day of the week with the Jews, and not the first day as with us) Christ went to the church in Capernaum, and taught in such a way that all felt the force of his words. But there was one man there who felt more than all the rest. It was a mad man, who had, as the Jews thought, a fiend in him, which drove him to do all sorts of bad things. He came to church that day (a strange place for a man who had a fiend in him, to go!) and when he heard Christ preach he could not bear it. He cried out, with a loud voice, " Let us be! What have we to do with thee, Jesus of Nazareth? Art thou come to put an end to us? I know thee who thou art, the HOLY ONE of God."

" Hold thy peace and come out of him," says Jesus. As his firm gaze meets the wild eyes of the poor mad man, he yields to his strong will and the will of God. The fiend comes out of him, and the man is left weak and faint, but his mind is sound now; he is a new man. It is not strange that the fame of this great deed should have spread far and near.

" Who can this be (all men say who were at church that day, or heard what was done there) whom the fiends mind at once? Who makes them let fall their prey, and fly at a mere word from his lips?"

When church was out, Christ and two or three of his friends went home with Peter to his house.

They had not been there long when he was told that there was some one sick in the house.

The good Grand-Ma of the house lies sick. Jesus goes to her bed, takes her by the hand, lifts her up, and she is well at once! so well that she goes right to work to get up a nice feast for him who has brought her back to life, and for his friends. But there is not much rest for Christ that day. As soon as the sun is down (the Jews' day of rest lasts from the hour when the sun sets one day, till it sets the next) a strange crowd flock to Peter's door. The whole town came, Mark says. The sick of all sorts are brought to him who taught in the church that day, and made the mad man well.

He heals all who come, and casts out not a few fiends from those who have been vext by them a long time. What a scene it must have been!

The great crowd of old and young, sick and well, mad and sane. At first there would be cries for help on all sides; the groans of the sick; the shrieks of the mad.

But as Jesus stands in the door, and his kind eyes glance from cot to cot, from group to group, and from face to face, all grows still. The sick feel their pains pass from them; the minds of the mad come back to them; the peace of God falls on all.

Think how much Christ did in this one short day, and yet, much as he needs rest, he does not spend much time in sleep. He knows the crowd will come back the next day, and he steals out, at dawn, to find some nook where he can pray. But Peter soon finds him, and tells him, "All men seek for thee." But he has done as much for Capernaum as he thinks it best to do just now.

"Let us go to the next towns," he says, "that I may preach there too; for that is what I came to the world to do." He has but three years in which to work, and one town must not keep him all the time.

In one town to which Jesus went on this tour, he had a new case brought to his view.

There were some sick ones in that land which no skill of man could cure. Those who were sick in this way gave up all hope. They had to give up their homes and their friends, too. They were so sick that I can't bear to tell you of it. They could still walk up and down the streets, but all who met them shrank from them, they were so foul to look at.

A man who was sick in this way heard that Jesus was in town, and had wrought great cures. He could not hear that Jesus had as yet made one who had this worst ail of all well, yet he knew that in old times Elisha had wrought a cure on Naaman, who had it, and from all he had heard of Christ, he was sure he was still more great than Elisha. So he made his way to Christ, and knelt at his feet, and cried, "If thou wilt, thou canst make me clean!"

Jesus did not shrink back from the poor man's foul face. Ah, no! his eyes are full of love as he looks at him. He lays his soft hand on the rough vile flesh, and says, "I will;

be thou clean!" Oh, how that man must have felt, to know that he was once more clean! That the vile skin which made all hate to look at him, and which made him hate his own self, had gone, and in its stead was the fair, smoooth skin of a child!

He was so glad, and made such a stir in the town as he told the good news from street to street, that Christ had to leave the town and go out in the fields. Jesus came to save men's souls far more than to heal the sick. But his cure of this sick man had made all who knew of it so wild, that they were in no state of mind to hear him preach. They would want more "signs," and not sit at his feet to be taught of Him. So he dare not stay there, but goes from them to some lone spot. But there the crowd find him, and flock to him from all sides.

In a few days, we hear of him as back in Capernaum. As soon as the news spreads that he has come home, such a crowd come to see and hear him that there is no room that can hold them all, and the street is full of them. While he speaks to this great crowd, he sees four men who try to push their way to him. They bring a sort of cot, on which lies a poor man who has lost the use of all his limbs. They push this way and that, but the press is so great that they can not get to the door with their load. But a bright thought strikes them. They can get to the steps which lead up to the roof of Christ's house. So they climb up there with the sick man.

Then they set down the bed, and pull off the rim which runs round the edge of the roof, and then bind him tight in his bed, and let him down by means of ropes to the court yard of the house. Jesus was glad to see them take such pains for their friend, and glad, too, that they had such faith in Him. So he made haste to aid them. But he saw that the sick man's soul was worse off than his limbs, so he made that well first. " Son! I blot out thy sins!" said he.

In the crowd are some scribes who thought they knew all there was to know of the things of God. They have not come to be taught, but to find fault. When they heard these words which Christ would have no right to speak had he not been the

Son of God, their minds are full of dark thoughts. But Christ reads their hearts, and knows all their thoughts as well as if they spoke.

"Why do you think these things in your hearts?" he says to the scribes. "He who has the right to blot out sins, can, of course, give strength to the man's limbs. I will prove this to you."

So he turns to the sick man (who still lies on his bed with no more use of his limbs than if they had been cut off), and says, "Rise, take up thy bed and go thy way to thy own house!"

He rose at once, took up his cot, and went off with it with strong limbs and a clean heart!

The crowd make way for the well man, as they would not for the sick, and he and his four friends who have lost their load in such a strange way, go home to tell the good news, and all praise God for what has been done.

One day, as Christ went through the gate of the town, he saw a man who sat there to take toll on the goods that were brought in, and see that all should pay the tax which Rome laid on all men and all goods. Those who took tolls in this way, were apt to get rich, but they lost caste with the rest of the Jews. All Jews felt it as a great shame and grief that the yoke of Rome was on their necks, and they did not like to have one of their own race work for those whose slaves they were. But Christ saw in this man, whose name was Matthew, one to love and not to hate. He bade him

less times than the scribes think right. These scribes were so sharp as to the times when a man should wash, and as to whom he should eat and drink with, and how he should stand when he went to pray, and how he should turn out his toes when he went to walk, and such like things, that they let slip all thought of what the state of the heart was.

They did not care how full of hate and all bad things a man's heart might be, if his hands and feet were made to move in just that way which they had made up their minds was the right way.

The fear of the scribes was not that Christ would break God's law, but their laws.

The next cure which Christ wrought

was done in church, on God's day of rest. A man was there whose hand was dried up, so that it was of no use to him. It may be these foes of Christ who, as I told you, were on the watch, had brought him there as a sort of trap for Christ. At least they are there, and ask Christ at once if he thinks it right to cure a man on that day. What scorn he must have felt for these mean men who thus try to catch him! But he does not crush them with a look, as he might have done; he just says, "Who is there of you who, if his sheep should fall in a pit on this day, would not pull it out? Is not a man worth more than a sheep? So it is right to do well on God's day."

Then he turns to the poor man, whose hand hangs like a dry stick at his side, and says, "Stretch forth thy hand!" he does so, and at once the red blood flows through its veins, and it is a firm, good hand once more.

Were these spies glad? No; they go out with a scowl of hate, to plot how they may kill Jesus!

We next hear of Christ as gone out from the town to a mount, where he prays all night long. He has a great work to do the next day; no less a work than to choose twelve men from out the band of friends which cling to him.

These are to be his school whom he is to teach, as he can not teach the crowd who come and go, and he will leave his work in charge of these when he dies. Mark says that he chose them that they might be with him, and that he might send them forth to preach, and to heal the sick, and to cast out fiends.

The names of the twelve were :

| | |
|---|---|
| SIMON PETER, | THOMAS, |
| ANDREW, | LEVI (or MATTHEW, |
| JAMES, | JAMES 2ND, |
| JOHN, | THADDEUS (or LEB- |
| PHILIP, | BEUS), |
| NATHANAEL (or BAR- | SIMON 2ND, |
| THOLOMEW), | JUDAS ISCARIOT. |

All of these, but Judas, were from Galilee.

By the time that Christ had made choice of the twelve, great crowds had found out where he was, and came out to seek him. If I were you, I would learn by heart the words which Jesus spoke to that great throng that day, with the green slope of the Mount for his church. You will find them in Matthew 5th, 6th and 7th.

When he went back to the town it was not to rest, though he had had none for long, long hours.

There were troops in the town, and at the head of them was a man who, though not a Jew, had won the love of the Jews. He had made the yoke of Rome as light as he could, and had gone so far in his kind deeds as to have built a church for the Jews of the town.

Now this man had a slave who was most dear to him, and who lay at the point of death. He had heard of Jesus and the cures he had wrought, and wants his help, but he shows that he is a well bred man, and has great tact in the way he takes to send for Christ. He does not send a slave from his house, nor some of the five score men in his troop. He asks some of the chief of the Jews (whom he made his friends when he built their church) to go for him and beg Jesus to come to his aid.

These Jews plead the case so well that Christ goes with them.

When the group had got near the house, he at whose call Christ had come, sent friends to meet him, and say, "Lord, do not take so much pains for me! I am not fit that thou shouldst come to my house. I did not think I was fit to go and ask thee to do this great thing for me. But say the word, and I know my slave will live. As I send my men from post to post, say to this one, ' go here,' and to that one, ' go there,' so I know that thou canst send life and health where thou wilt."

Christ, when he hears these words, looks at the group who stand with him, his own near friends, as well as the proud old Jews and the throng who have come to join them on the way, and says, " I say to you all, that I have not seen such great faith as this ; no, not in Israel!" and when the friends get back to the house they find the sick man well!

The next day Christ went to the town of Nain. This town was eight hours walk from Capernaum, and as Christ and his friends drew near the gate, they met a long train which brought forth a dead man to lay him in the grave. As they stood to let the train pass by, Jesus caught sight of one face whose woe went right to his heart. It was the face of her whose child that dead man was. Her one child and her all.

Two years from this time Jesus will look down from his own death bed, the cross, and see just such a face as that on the ground at its foot. Mary will be there thrust through with the sword which old Simeon told her would pierce her heart. Jesus has to die to save a world, and so can not give Mary back her own son, but he will give her his best friend to be her son in his stead.

It would not be strange if the thought of this scene, in which he was so soon to bear a part, should have been in the mind of Him who knew all things, at this time. But here is a son whom he can give back to her whose one staff he is.

"Weep not!" he says to her.

He draws near and lays his hand on the bier. Those who bear it set it down, and the whole long train stop and stare at this strange check. Then said he to the dead man, whose grave waits for him but a few steps off, "Young man, I bid thee rise!" He who speaks these words is a young man like him who lies there, cold and dead; but at his words life comes back to the dead man, love to his heart, and words come to his lips. He sits up on the bier and speaks, and Christ gives the son back to the arms of her who thought she had held him there for the last time.

This is the first time that Jesus gave life to the dead, and " there came a fear on all."

The news spreads far and wide, till it gets to the ears of John Baptist. We have not heard of him for a long time. The truth is he has been for some months shut up in a strong fort down by the Dead Sea. It was the rage to hear John Baptist preach at one time, you know. The king heard of him, and sent for him to preach at court, or else drove out to the wilds where he dwelt to hear him. But Herod heard no smooth words from him. What does John care for the crown of that bad man who sits to hear what new thing he has to say? All he sees in him is sin, and that sin is not made less in his eyes, but far worse, by the fact that it is done by a king.

Herod did not dare kill John on the spot, for the Jews would not have borne that, but he shuts him up in that strong fort of his.

It seems that John could see his friends, and that they went back and forth from the world to him and told him the news.

When John hears that Christ has gone so far as to raise the dead, he seems to think that the right time has come for him to prove that he is the Son of God. It is hard to wait when one's hands are tied so he can not work at all. It may be John thinks it strange that Christ does not set him free; at least he sends two of his friends, who have stood by him in spite of his chains, to ask Christ point blank, "Art thou He that should come, or must we still look for Him?" He did not say yes or no to them; he said more than yes. He gave proof on proof that he was he that should come. "Go your way; tell John what things ye have seen and heard; how the blind see, the lame walk, the sick are made well, the deaf hear, the dead rise up to life, and the poor at last hear the good news of God." But Christ adds, "he is best who holds fast his faith in me, in spite of all that looks most dark."

There was a sect in that day who thought they were the cream of the world. No one was half so good as they, they were quite sure. One of this proud class thought he would ask

Christ to dine with him, and see what he could make of him.

Christ goes to the proud man's feast, just as he would go to a poor man's house. It is all one to him, for he looks at the man and not at his things. But this proud Simon is not a well bred host, as we shall soon hear Christ tell him.

Christ takes his seat at the board. They did not sit on chairs when they ate, as we do. They half lay on a couch, with the feet thrown back.

While Christ sat at meat, there crept in one who has heard that he is a guest there. She stoops down by the couch, and her tears flow forth at the sight of his pure face and the thought of her bad life. Her tears fall in such floods that she bathes the dust from Christ's feet with them, and then wipes them with her long hair, which has been her pride; and gives kiss on kiss to those way worn feet. Then she takes a box of choice balm worth its weight in gold, and pours it out on his feet, that she may cool and rest them.

Simon sees all this, and knows her who kneels there too well.

He says not a word, but there is a sneer on his proud face, as he thinks in his heart, " Oh! I've found him out! He is not what the mob take him to be, or he would shrink back from the touch of her who kneels at his feet, for he would know what a bad life hers has been." But the voice of Christ breaks on his ear.

" Simon, I have a word for thee."

' Say on," says the host, who does

not dream that his heart has been read like a book by him who speaks.

"Two men are in debt to one lord. This one owes him a small sum, and that one ten times as much. As both of them have no means with which to pay him, their lord wipes out the score of both, and frees them from the debt. Now which of them will feel the most love for the lord who has been so kind to them?"

Simon does not see the point, but says, "Why, I should think that he who had been most in debt would love him most."

"You are right," says Christ to his host, and then he turns to her who weeps at his feet, and says, "Simon, do you see her who kneels here? I came to your house, but you sent no one to bathe the dust from my feet, but she pours out her own tears to wash them, and wipes them with the hair of her own head.

"When I came in, you did not give me the kiss on the cheek with which a host in our land is wont to greet his guests, but she rains kiss on kiss on my feet, and has done so with no pause since I came in! You brought no oil for my head, as is the way at our feasts, but she pours out on my feet her choice balm. For this cause I say to you, I will blot out all her sins, though they are, as you think them, and as she thinks them, not few; for she loves much. But he who thinks he does not owe much will not feel much love to him who frees him from the debt." Then, with a look full of love on the poor soul at his feet, he said, " I blot out thy sins; thy faith saves thee; go in peace."

New friends now join Christ in his tour from town to town. One of them at least, is of high rank. Her name was Joanna, and she was the wife of Chuza, who was a lord of Herod's court.

Mary Magdalene was with him, too, and not a few of her sex who had been won to Christ by his cures and his words of grace. We have cause to think that these kind friends staid with him till the end of his life, and we know that some of them were the last to leave his tomb when he was laid there, and the first to see him when he rose from it.

One day, when Christ had spent

the day on the shore of the Sea of Tiberias, and had taught the crowds which came to him there till night had come, some of the twelve took him out in a ship, that he might get a chance to rest. He was worn out by his toil, and soon he slept.

While he lay at rest, a great storm came down on the lake. Though the lake is not large, yet strong gusts of wind from the hills sweep down at times and make it foam and rage, so it is at the risk of life that one sails on it. The winds roar and the waves toss, but still Jesus sleeps. At last the waves sweep through the boat, and then the crew in their fright run to him and wake him from his sleep with their cries.

"Dost thou not care that we are

lost! Lord, save, or we shall be lost!"

He wakes at once, and chides first them, and then the winds and the waves. To them who have seen sight come to the blind, health to the sick, life to the dead, by his mere word, he says, " Why are you so full of fears? where is your faith?" and to the sea, which leaps up to the prow of the ship on which he stands, and roars for its prey, he says, " Peace, be still!"

The winds and the waves sink at once, and there is a great calm on the sea. But in the hearts of those who are with him there is no calm. They gaze at him with new awe, and in spite of all the great signs they have seen from him in days past, they ask, " Who can this be who can make the wind and the sea mind him!" It took them so long to learn that Christ could do all things.

At dawn of day the ship comes to the shore, and they land near the town of Gadara. As they touch the shore a mad man flies to meet them. He is so wild that no one dares to pass that way. He haunts the place of tombs, wears no clothes, and no man can bind him; no, not with chains. He has been bound with chains at times, but he breaks them off as if they had been of flax. By night and day he haunts this wild spot, and makes the rocks ring with his cries, as he cuts his flesh with the stones.

His fierce eye sees Christ when he is yet far off, and he runs to meet him, and bows down at his feet, and cries, " What have I to do with thee, Jesus, thou Son of the most high God?"

Jesus, who has just laid the storm to rest by a word, now brings peace to this poor soul where the fiends have dwelt so long. He bids them come out of him and vex him no more. There is a herd of swine in the fields near them, and the fiends beg that they may go to them when they leave the man. As soon as they do so, the great herd run mad and plunge down a steep place to the sea, which drowns them all.

The men who had charge of the swine fled, and told all whom they met by the way and in the town, what had been done. A crowd flock out to the shore to see the sight.

There is Jesus, and at his feet sits that fierce mad man who has been their dread so long; but he is not mad now. He is in his right mind, and his eyes, as they gaze on the face of him who has made him once more a man, and not a band of fiends, are full of love and awe!

You think, do you not, that all who came out and saw that sight must have cried to Jesus to bless them too? That they would beg him to go back to their town and heal the sick, and cast out fiends, and bless their homes with the light of his dear face? But they do not; no, they pray him to leave their coasts!

There is, to be sure, a man right in their sight whose soul is his own once more, but then there are all those dead pigs! It will not do to risk our stock for the sake of a few souls more. So Christ turns his back on them, and goes back to the ship. He will force his grace on no one. The man whom he has made sane and sound clings to him, and begs to go with him. But Christ says no, and sends him to tell the tale and show the proof of what has been done for him. "Go home to thy friends, and tell them how great things God hath done for thee." And so he goes to preach Christ up and down the streets of the ten towns of Decapolis.

When Christ got back to his own shore once more, he found a great throng who were on the watch for him, and while he spoke to them, a man made his way through the throng and knelt at Jesus' feet. All knew him, for it is Jairus, who rules a church in Capernaum, and is much thought of in the town. He begs Jesus to go home with him, where his one dear child, a girl twelve years old, lies at the point of death.

"I pray thee come and lay thy hands on her, and she shall live!" he says, in his strong faith.

Jesus rose at once and went with him. The crowd go too, and more and more join them as they go on. In the midst of them is one who has been sick for twelve long years. She has spent all she had on men of skill who thought they could cure her, but all in vain, for she grew worse and worse. She lost all hope of help long since, but now she hears of Jesus, and the great cures he has wrought, and is sure if she can but touch the fringe of his robe, it will make her well. She does not wish that he should see her, so she creeps up and puts out her hand that she may touch and fly. The touch makes her well! and with a heart full of joy she gives way to the crowd, and thinks no one knows what great thing has been done to her. But at once Jesus turns on the crowd, and asks whose touch it was which he had felt.

Peter, who is apt to speak first, says, "How can you ask whose touch it was when there is such a crowd on all sides?"

But Jesus says that the touch of faith has been felt by him, and a cure has been wrought in the crowd. He does not ask for his own sake, for he knows right well who it was, but he wants to do still more for her, and make her faith firm as a rock. His eye finds her in all the crowd, and she who yet so thrills with what has been done in her, sees that she can not be hid, and falls down at his feet, and tells him and the crowd the whole tale. " My child, be of good cheer, thy faith hath made thee whole; go in peace." I think when she heard those words she must have been quite glad that Jesus did not let her creep off home, as she tried to do!

When Christ makes us well, we should tell all whom we know of it, that they too may go to him in their needs.

But this scene, brief as it was, kept

back Jesus on his way to the sick child, and while he yet talks with her who kneels at his feet, the sad news comes to Jairus, "It is of no use to seek help, thy child is dead."

That must have been a great shock to poor Jairus, but Jesus is at hand to hold him up. "Fear not," Jesus says to him; "If you have but faith, she shall be made whole." So they press on to the house. They find a crowd there.

Some are friends, and some are the men whom it is the way of the land to hire, in case of death, to weep and wail and make all the noise they can. The more rich a man is, the more of these mock tears and groans he can hire! Jairus was a man of rank, so the noise was great in the house where the dear child lay in the sleep of death. Christ would let none of the crowd go in with him but Peter and James and John, and bade those who cried with such a loud noise, " Give place! the maid is not dead, but sleeps."

Their mock tears change to a laugh of scorn at these words, for they know that she is dead. But Christ put them all out, and took no one in the room of death but Jairus and his wife, and and his own three friends. There she lies, her face white and still in death. She has not heard the din of those who mourn for hire; she does not see the tears of those who now stand by the bed of their sweet child, half in fear and half in hope. But she does hear at once the voice of Jesus. He speaks but two words in the Jews' tongue: " Rise, child!" Her soul comes back, she starts up from her bed, she walks, and Christ bids them give her food.

As soon as Jesus had left the house of Jairus, two blind men heard that he was near, and made their way to his house with him. As they went through the streets they cried, " Thou son of David! Thou son of David, help us!" But Jesus did not heal them till he got home. Then he said to them, " Have you faith that I can do this for you?"

They said, " Yes, Lord."

Then he laid his hand on their eyes and said, "As is your faith, so be it to you."

We know how great their faith must have been, for their blind eyes saw once more, and they went out to spread the fame of him who gave them sight.

There seems to have been no rest for Christ that day. As soon as the blind men were gone, a new group of friends came to his door for aid. They have with them a man who is in a sad state. He has a fiend in him, and is dumb. Christ does not ask for faith in this poor soul, but heals him for the sake of those whose faith has brought him there. He casts out the fiend, and the dumb man speaks. All cry that such a thing has not been known as that the dumb should speak. But that proud sect of which I told you, who thought they knew all there was to know, though they dare not say Christ could not cast out fiends at all,

CHRIST RESTORES THE BLIND TO SIGHT

said he did it by the help of the prince of fiends!

Christ next goes once more to his old home in Nazareth. He will give them one more chance to own him and let him bless them, as they must have heard he has done all the towns where he has been.

They have heard all this, and they see the crowds that go with Jesus in all his tours, but they have no more faith than when he first came to them. "We know him too well. We knew him as a child. Some of his kin still dwell in our town. There can not be much to him!"

They do not dare mob him, as they had done the first time he came to them, for he has too large a band of friends with him. But they greet him with frowns and not with smiles, and all he can do for that poor, mean town, is to lay his hand on a few sick folk and heal them, for they have no faith in him.

Christ now made his third tour through Galilee, to teach and preach and heal, from town to town. But when he saw the great flocks who came out to hear him, and saw how much need they had of some one to guide them and teach them, his heart was drawn out by the sight. He said they were like lost sheep, faint for want of food, and with no one to lead them to the fold. He knew that he could not be long with them. His time on earth was short, and he must soon leave them, and go to coasts where he had not yet been seen.

So he sent the twelve out, two by two, to help him in his great work. He gave them the right and the strength to preach, to heal the sick, raise the dead, and to cast out fiends. They were to take no robe with them but that they wore, no goods, or purse, or food. They were just to go, staff in hand, from town to town, and take what fare they could find.

He bade them preach where they could, and when they found a town which did not wish to hear them, they were to go from it at once, and shake off the dust of their feet as a sign that the curse of God was on them for their scorn of His grace.

But he told the twelve that they would have a hard time. That they would be like sheep in the midst of wolves, and must be on their guard all the time. They were to prove by their words and deeds that they were both wise and free from guile. He bade them make up their minds to stand in courts and face kings, and feel the scourge and win the hate of all men; and all this for the sake of Christ their Lord. But to cheer them he told them that God, who took such care of the least of birds, that one of them could not fall to the ground and He not see it, would care for them who were far more dear. And, most of all, that He would count all that was done to them as if it were done to him.

Christ did not rest while the twelve went out on their tour. He, too, went on with his work from town to town. While the twelve are gone from him, the news is brought him that John Baptist is dead. We left John in Herod's fort. While there he seems to have won the king's good will in spite of his bold thrusts at his sins. When he heard him preach, the king did not a few things, and heard him with joy. He tried to patch up his bad life here and there, but did not give up the one black sin which John told him he must get rid of. His wife is one whom it was a sin for him to take, but he still keeps her.

Her heart is full of hate when she finds that she can not make the king kill this bold man who chides him for his sin. She plots how she can put her foe to death, and as she knows Herod's weak points so well, she soon finds a time and a way.

Herod's birth day has come, and a gay feast has been held in the court. Herodias (that is the bad wife's name) has a child who is as full of wiles as she. Her name is Salome.

Herodias sends her in, when the feast is at its height, to dance a wild, free dance, in the hall where the feast is kept.

Herodias knows what the king is when he is mad with wine.

She hears with joy the wild shouts which he and his lords send up as Salome, bold bad girl that she was, leaps and glides to and fro in the mad dance.

It turns out as Herodias knew it would. Herod, drunk, says, with an oath, that he will give a girl who can dance like that, just what she asks.

Herodias tells her what to ask. What fair, choice thing can it be that a young girl can ask for a gift? The head of John the Baptist!

"I will that thou give me, by and by, the head of John the Baptist in a dish!"

Do you want to know more of a girl like that?

Herod has so much sense left in spite of his wine, as to feel a pang of grief that he has been caught in such a trap, and he longs to save the just man's life. But his oath, though he took it when he was drunk, is more in his eyes than God's law. He sends at once to the fort, and the grim head with its sad eyes and long locks, is soon brought in, and the girl takes the dish which holds it, and trips out with her prize!

Those who have clung to John the Baptist, in spite of his chains, take up his corse and lay it in the grave, and then go right to Jesus with the sad tale.

But Herod is not at ease. The fumes of the feast have gone off, and the thought that he has slain a good brave man, haunts the king like his ghost. He is so ill at ease, that when he hears of a young man who goes from town to town with signs and great deeds, he is full of fears. He says, "It is true that I cut off the head of John the Baptist, but who but he can this be who can do such things? This is John the Baptist who has come to life once more."

He did not guess that he was more than John, that he was the Judge of

John, and of Herod, and of all the world, at whose bar he shall one day stand and hear his doom, from the lips of him whom he now wants to see.

When the twelve came back from their tour, Christ went with them in search of a place of rest, where the crowd could not find them. They went by boat to the shore near Bethsaida, but though they went to get free from the crowds, they fail.

The crowds find out where they have gone, and run out to meet them, and Christ must preach and heal, and not rest.

It is spring now, near the time of the feast, so that trains are on their way down to Jerusalem, which makes the throng still more great. It is near night, and Jesus sees that the hosts of old and young who have come so far to hear him, need food.

Philip is there, whose home is close at hand in Bethsaida, and so Christ turns to him and asks, "Where shall we buy bread that these may eat?"

"This he said to prove Philip," it is said, "for He knew what He would do."

Philip does not think of Christ's might; he thinks how great the crowd is, and how small a sum they have in their purse which Judas has charge of. All the twelve, too, ask Christ to send the great throng off to buy food and find a place to lodge. But Jesus says, "They need not go: give ye them to eat!"

The twelve stare at him, and then beg to know if they are to go and buy the loads of bread which it will take to give each one of the vast throng the least bit to eat.

"How much bread have you? go and see."

They tell him that there is a lad there who has five loaves and two small fish; "but what are they to feed such a host of men as are here?"

They count the loaves, you see, but do not count Christ. He does not chide them for their want of faith, but calls for the bread and the fish to be brought him. Then he bids the twelve make them sit down in ranks on the green grass. Those who count them, say there are ten times ten rows, and two score and ten men in each row; but do not count the wives and young folks who were to be fed as well as the men. When the ranks are in place, and all is still as they wait for Christ's word, he takes the bread and fish and gives thanks.

You must not think of these five loaves, as like the great loaves of New England bread, or like that of France, which you can buy by the yard. They are small, thin cakes, and the fish, too, are small, which Christ holds in his hands and deals out to the twelve, but there seems to be no end to them!

The twelve pass to and fro through the ranks with the food, and all eat their fill, and yet, when not a child can call for one more bit, there is so much left as will fill twelve of the sacks which those who have set out for the Feast have with them! Far more is left when all are fed, than all that they had at first to eat!

This moves the crowd more than all the signs they have seen him do. " How grand it would be to have a king who could feed us all the time like this, and take care of us! We could lie on the green sward and hear him talk, and have no hard tax to pay to Rome, and no hard work to do!"

· But when Christ saw that they would come and take him by force to make him a king, he sent the twelve to their ship, and then sent the crowd to find a place to lodge, but he went to a mount to pray. But the twelve do not get on well while their Lord is gone. A sharp gust comes down on the lake from the hills, and drives their ship up and down at its will.

They do their best to steer for the safe port of Capernaum, and toil at the oars, but all in vain. Day is at hand, for it is past three o'clock, and yet with all their hard work through the long night they have not gone three miles. In this strait they see a strange sight. In the dim light they see the form of a man out on the broad lake. The waves leap and foam, but he glides on as if his feet trod a smooth green lawn.

They cry out with fear. They do not think of Christ till they hear his voice, which they know so well, say, " Be of good cheer! It is I. Do not fear."

Peter grows bold at this, and cries to the Lord as he draws near, " If it be thou, bid me come to thee on the sea!" " Come!"

CHRIST REBUKING PETER.

So Peter leaps down from the ship and steps out with quite a brave air. But the wind blows, and the waves rise to meet him, and he looks at them and not at Christ, and so, of course, he sinks. His faith is not so strong as his fears. But as he sinks he cries to Christ, " Lord, save me!"

Christ's hand grasps the strong man, so weak of heart, and holds him up, and the two are soon safe on board the ship. When Christ stands on the deck, the winds cease to blow, and all on board fall at his feet and say, " On a truth thou art the Son of God."

They do not land at Capernaum, but some miles south of that port, on the shore of Gennesareth. As soon as it is known that Jesus is there, all the sick are brought out from their homes, and all are made well if they but touch the hem of his robe.

When Christ gets back to Capernaum he finds the whole town in a stir.

The crowd which he had fed the last night on the hill side, have sought him in vain on that shore, and have come here to find out where he can be. But as they tell the strange tale of how he fed them, they hear that he is on this side the lake. They know that the twelve went off in all the the boat there was on that side, and that Christ did not go with them, and yet here he is in the church at Capernaum!

"Lord, when didst thou come here?" they cry, as he stands up to preach. They want to hear of more signs and strange things which he has done, but he turns on them with plain words.

"Ye seek me just for the sake of the bread and the fish which ye ate! But it is your souls which need food. Do not spend the strength of your lives just to get bread to fill your mouths; but seek for that bread that will give life to your souls, life that shall have no end."

Then they say, "Lord, give us that bread."

"I am that bread; I am the bread of life. He that comes to me shall want no more; and he that has faith in me shall thirst no more. But you have seen me and have not faith."

How well he knew their hearts! Just then a buzz goes round the church as they find fault with his words.

"How dare he say that he is the bread of life, and come down from on high, when we know so well whose son he is?"

But Christ once more says the same words, and adds those which are still more hard to bear.

"I am the Bread of Life which came down from on high. He who eats of this bread shall live as long as God lives."

Then comes the buzz once more, "How can this man give us his flesh to eat?"

"If you do not eat the flesh of the Son of man and drink his blood, ye have no life in you. He who eats my flesh and drinks my blood shall have the life that shall not end." This is too much to bear. They had come to hear of a great king who will save them from the hands of their foes, and make them rich, and strong, and grand, as they were in the best old times. But they hear in place of plans for such an end as this, strange words which speak of death; of torn flesh and spilt blood.

Some who had been most with him, and had long sat in his school, now go and leave him, to walk with him no more.

Then said Jesus to the twelve, " Will you leave me too?"

Peter speaks the best words we have heard from him yet: " Lord, to whom can we go? Thou hast the words of life. We think—yes, we know that thou art the Christ the Son of God!"

Christ must have bent a look of love on Peter when he hears these warm words, but he has one more "hard" word for this small group who Peter is sure will cling to him though all leave him. They do not know their own hearts, but he does, and says, " Did I not choose twelve of you, and one of you is a fiend?"

Christ has now come to the last year of his life. He seeks a place of rest, and goes to the north, to the coasts of Tyre and Sidon. The twelve have shown that they care for his words no less than his works, and Christ wants to take them where they can be free for a time from the crowds who come to stare and find fault. But he can not be hid.

There is a Greek in that land, who has heard of the cures wrought by Jesus. She has a child who is vext by a fiend, and comes to the house where Jesus and the twelve are guests, and cries for help. Her cries do not touch the hearts of the twelve. She is not a Jew, and what right has she to ask help of their Lord? They have yet to learn that Christ came to save a world, and not just that small nook of it where the Jews dwell. They bid Christ to send her off, for she will not mind them. To prove her faith, and, it may be, quite as much to shame the twelve, he acts as if he he did not mean to help her. But her love for her child is so great, and she is so sure that here is one who can help her, that no sharp words can drive her off. She clings to him still, till Christ cries to her, " O, great is thy faith! Be it to thee as thou wilt. The fiend has gone out of thy child!"

And when she got home the fiend was gone, and her own dear child was there to greet her!

On his way back to the Sea of Galilee, Christ went through those ten towns which bore the name of Decapolis. He had been here but once, and that was the time when a man was made whole and a herd of swine lost. But they do not ask him to leave now. They brought to him a man who was deaf, and who was tongue tied, and he makes him hear and speak, and the news spreads, till a host, who need help, flock to him. The lame, blind, dumb, and the sick of all sorts are brought and laid down at his feet, and he heals them.

Once more he feeds a great throng with a few small cakes of bread and a few fish, and then goes home to Galilee.

He next went to Bethsaida, where a blind man was brought to him. At Christ's first touch he sees men as if they were trees; but at the next, all things are clear to his sight.

As Christ and the twelve are on their way to Cæsarea Philippi, he talks with them by the way of what men say of him.

They tell him that some say he is John the Baptist, and some that he is this or that great man of old, who has come back to the earth.

"But whom do you say I am?"

Peter cries, "Thou art the Christ, the Son of God!"

Then Jesus tells them, in words that are much more plain than he has made use of till now, that the Son of man must go to Jerusalem, and bear great wrongs; he must be cast out by the chief priests and the scribes, be put to death, and rise from the grave on the third day.

Peter is too bold now. He takes it on him to chide Christ for this course which he has laid out for his own feet: "Be it far from thee, Lord! this shall not be!"

He, too, wants to see Christ reign with the pomp and show of one of the kings of earth, and has yet to learn that through the cross lies Christ's path to a crown which shall last, and be more and more bright when all the kings of earth are dust, and when the earth has come to an end.

Jesus speaks sharp words to Peter, and then bids all who hear him know once for all, that they who want to be His, must take up their cross each day, and walk in the path of toil and pain which His own feet have made for them.

But he tells them that the Son of man will one day come in his might with the hosts of God. And when he shall come, he will make up to his friends for all the loss and shame they have borne for him, and put to shame all who have not been true to him in spite of the scorn of the world.

In a few days from the time when

this talk was held, Jesus took with him Peter, James and John, and went up to a mount to pray. While they are there they are made glad with a glimpse of their Lord in that form which he will wear when we shall all see him, as we hope, in his joy.

They have slept, we know not how long, while Jesus prays. When they wake, they see three bright forms. The chief is their Lord. His face shines like the sun, and his robes are white, like the light. With him stand Moses and Elias, and the three talk of the death by which Christ will soon, at Jerusalem, win life for us all.

Then Peter, who is in such a daze that he does not know what he says, cries, "It is good for us to be here! If thou wilt, let us build here three homes; one for thee, one for Moses, and one for Elias!"

But while he speaks, a bright cloud rests on the top of the mount, and from it is heard a voice which says, " This is my dear Son; hear ye him," and Peter and his mates fall on the ground in fear, for they know they have heard the voice of God.

But at Christ's touch they rise, the bright scene is past, they see no one but Jesus. As they come down from the mount with him, he bids them tell no one what they have seen, till he shall rise from the dead.

The first sight they meet when they reach the foot of the mount, is one of sin and woe. In the midst of the crowd who wait for Christ, is a poor man with his son, all the child he has.

This son is mad—torn by a fiend, they say. The fiend drives him where it will. At times it burns him, and at times drowns him. It tears him and makes him foam at the mouth, and gnash with the teeth, and he pines to death. " Lord look on my son!" cries the poor man. I brought him to these friends of thine who have been taught to preach and heal by thee, but they could not cast out the fiend. Lord, if thou canst, O help us!"

" It is if THOU canst" Christ says; " If thou canst have faith."

Then the man cries out, with tears, " Lord, I have some faith; help thou my want of faith."

Christ calls to the fiend which plagues the boy, " Thou deaf and dumb fiend, come out of him!" Then the fiend cried, and rent the boy sore, and came out of him, and he was as one dead; so that those that stood near said, "he is dead." But Jesus took him by the hand, and he rose up, and was well from that hour.

On the way back to Capernaum the twelve have a war of words as to which of them shall be chief! How it must have made their Lord's heart ache to hear them! He has just told them in such plain words that they can not doubt it, that he is soon to leave them by a death of woe, and yet they can waste the time in such strife as this! But Christ does not speak to them at the time. He waits till the heat of their strife is past, as we shall see.

When they reach Capernaum the

tax men come to Peter and say to him "Does not your lord pay a tax?" This tax was not for the king but the church tax. Peter did not wait to ask his Lord what he would have him say, but said "yes" at once. When Peter came in, Jesus did not wait for him to ask for the tax, but said "do the kings of the earth tax their own sons?" Peter says, "no." "Then are the sons free," What he meant was, that he as the son of God should not be made to pay a tax for God's house. "But," he adds, "lest we should vex them, go to the sea and cast a hook, and take up the first fish that comes. In his mouth you will find what will pay my tax and yours." At this same time Christ calls up the strife of the twelve by the way, and makes them hang their heads for shame. Then he says to them, " He who wants to be first, the same shall be last of all ; and shall serve all." To make this still more plain to them as he sits in the house, he calls a young child who is there and takes him up in his arms and says, this is what you must be or you can not find a place at all in my realm—not to speak of the chief place. He who shall be most like this child shall be chief in God's realm. Ah, dear child! what love Christ has for such as you! How can you but love him with all your heart, and strive, as you grow up, not to be great, but meek, and mild, and pure as the child whom Christ held in his arms that day?

The fall has now come and a great feast of the Jews draws near. This feast was meant to call to mind the time when they were on their way from Egypt to the good land where they now dwelt.

The law was, that they were all to leave their homes and camp out for this week of praise, in booths made of boughs. This must have been the best feast of the year, to the small folk at least.

Some of Christ's kin tried to make him go up to Jerusalem at this time, and do some great thing to prove that he was the king of the Jews. They had no true faith in him, which could wait for him to do his own work, in his own way and time. But he said, "Go ye up to this feast. I shall not go up yet, for my time is not yet full come."

So they went and left him.

At Jerusalem there was a great stir, and Jesus was the cause of it. All thought that he would be at the feast, but when they found he had not come he was the theme of all tongues. One told this thing he had done, and one told that. One said he was "a good man;" and one said, "no." But in the midst of the feast, all at once, Jesus stood in their sight, in the house of God, and taught. He knew that there were plots to kill him, but in the great throng who were now in Jerusalem he had not a few warm friends; and he would give those who were his foes a chance to hear his words of truth.

On the last day of the feast Jesus speaks once more in the house of God.

He tells all who have kept the feast, that they have seen a type of him each day of all the week of praise.

The high priest was wont to go to the Pool of Siloam and there fill a jar of gold, which he brought back to the house of God with great pomp. The great throng would meet him with palms in their hands, and a chant of praise. This would bring to mind the time when the tribes were faint with thirst, and when Moses smote the rock and a stream came forth to give them new life.

But this is what Jesus told them: "If a man thirst, let him come to me and drink! He that hath faith in me shall have a fount of life in his own soul, and shall not thirst."

These words go home to the hearts

of some who heard him, but some hate him all the more. That sect of the Jews which took the lead in all things, were full of hate of Christ. They were so proud and vain, that when they heard Christ teach that the way to please God was to be meek and mild, and like a child in heart, it drove them mad with rage. They and the chief priests sent men to take Christ and drag him to their court, where they could have their own way with him, and doom him to death. But when these men heard him preach they did not dare lay hands on him, for, as they said, "No man could speak like that!"

This made the rage of those who had sent them still more great. But there is in the midst of them one who has been for three years a friend to Christ at heart.

It is Nicodemus, the judge, who went long since to talk with Christ in the night. He now speaks for him, and says to his foes, " Doth our law judge a man who hath not been heard and his deeds well known?"

They turn on Nicodemus, and say, with a sneer, "Art thou, too, of Galilee?" but they do not at that time try to seize Jesus.

Christ spoke more than once in God's House while he was in Jerusalem at this time. More than once the mob, led on by the chief priests and scribes, cry out at his words, and once they take up stones to cast at him, but they can not harm him.

He cures one man, who was born

blind, and so had no hope of help from the skill of man.

Christ's foes try to think there is some trick here, and that the man was not blind. They call those whose son the blind man was, and press them to tell the whole tale. But they fear the court, and so all they will say is, " We know that this is our son, and that he was born blind; but by what means he now sees, or who made his eyes see, we know not. He is of age, ask him."

Then they call the man, and let him see at once what they want him to say. They bid him, " Give God the praise; and don't think that this man who we know is a bad man, could do such a great thing as to give sight to the blind."

But the man sticks to the truth:

"I know not," says he, "if he be a bad man or not; but I do know one thing, I was blind. Now I can see."

"But what did he do to you? How did he make you see?"

"I have told you, and you would not take my word for it; why do you want to hear it twice? Do you want to join his school too?"

Then they jeer and scoff. "We are of Moses' school," they say. "We know that God spake to Moses, but as for this man we know not from whence he is."

"That is most strange," said he who had been blind. "You who know all things, as you think, do not know who this man is who can do such a deed as to make a man see who was born blind! If he were not of God he could not have done this."

This turns their rage on the man, and they cut him off from the church; for they had said that a man who should own Jesus as the Christ, should be put out of the church.

When Jesus heard that he had been thus cast out by the Jews, he went to find him. When he had done so, he said to him, " Hast thou faith in the Son of God?"

" Who is he, Lord?"

Jesus said to him, " Thou hast seen him, and it is he who talks with thee now."

" Lord, I have faith in thee," he says, and falls at his feet.

Some months pass, and we do not know just where Christ spent all the time. He goes back to Jerusalem to a feast, but does not stay long. When he stands up to preach, the mob take up stones to stone him, and the court tries once more to take him. So he leaves the town and goes out to the banks of the Jordan. At this time he told not a few of those short tales which we all love to read so much, and which are meant for us as much as for those who first heard them.

You must read these in his own words.

The time now drew near when Jesus should leave the world.

As he is now to go up to Jerusalem for the last time, he means to go in such a way that all eyes will turn on him, and take note of the scenes through which he is to pass.

He makes choice of three score and ten men who have been taught in his school. These are to act as scouts, and see that the way is clear for Christ to walk in. They are told to go, two and two, to each town and place which lies on Christ's road to Jerusalem, and tell who had sent them. They are to heal the sick, but most of all, they are to warn those who hear them that Christ will soon pass through their streets with his gifts of grace.

In one town in Samaria. these scouts were met with frowns, and no place could be found for Christ there. They would have been glad to see him if they could have things in their own way, but Christ had said, in plain words, that he was on his way to Jerusalem, and Samaria's hate of Jerusalem was no less than Jerusalem's hate of Samaria.

When James and John saw this slight to their Lord, they were full of rage. They said, " Lord, wilt thou that we call for fire to come down from on high and put an end to them, as Elias did?"

But Christ chides them that they have not learnt more of his grace in all the time they have spent with him. " The Son of man is not come to take men's lives, but to save them," he said, and led them on. He will not force his grace on a town or a soul that does not wish for it.

One day they met a man who was so won by Christ's words that he said, " Lord, where thou dost go I will go with thee!"

Christ did not say, "Come!" to this man. He would have him count the cost ere he took such a step as that; so all he said to him was, "The fox hath his hole, and the bird of the air hath its nest; but the Son of man hath not where to lay his head."

Two more men whom Christ saw he bade come with him. Each had some things which it was his wish to do first, and then he said he would go with Christ. But Christ told them that his work must be first, and no one who set out to do it, who had once put his hand to the plough, must so much as look back.

It was on this last tour which Christ took with the train of friends, which had now grown to be so large, that one of those who heard him pray, said,

"Lord, teach us to pray as John taught his school."

And then Christ gave to them, and to us, those words, "Our Father," which we all make use of each day of our lives. And that we might have no doubt that it was right to pray, and that God would hear us and give us what we need, he told those who stood there who had sons of their own, that God had more love for them than they felt for their sons.

"If one of your sons ask you for bread, do you give him a stone? If he ask a fish, do you give him a snake?"

If you whose hearts are bad, know how to give good gifts to your child, how much more shall God, whose name is Love, give His best gifts to His child when he asks for them?

Ask and God will give to you; seek and you shall find.

There was one house where Christ was sure to find love and peace and rest. This was the home of Martha and Mary, and Lazarus, at Bethany. It was less than two miles from Jerusalem, so that Christ could walk there when the toils of the day were at an end, and find smiles of love, and kind words and deeds from the three who dwelt there, in place of the frowns and threats of the mob in the great town. There are proofs that this was a home of wealth, and that the three who dwelt here were much thought of in the town, as well as dear to Christ. At one time when Christ sought rest in this house Martha and Mary show out their traits in a strong light, and though it is said that Christ loves both, yet he seems in this case to praise Mary and chide Martha.

Mary shows her joy that he has come in her way, and Martha, whose love and joy are quite as strong, shows them in her own way. But Christ likes Mary's way the best. Martha wants to make a grand feast for him, but Mary sits at his feet to have her soul fed with the bread of life. Martha as she went in and out with her head full of plans for the feast, and her hands full of cares, lost much of the good of Christ's stay with them. She had a strong wish to make much of Christ, and show him that she did so, but it must be in her own way. Mary read Christ's heart best, and knew that he did not care for rich food and grand shows. His meat and drink were to do the will of him who sent him. He is in haste, as the time draws near for him to leave the world, to make known more of the great truths which he came to teach, and is glad to find a heart like Mary's which longs to learn all he longs to teach. When Martha asks him if he does not care that she is at work so hard, while Mary sits there with hands at rest, to drink in his words, Christ chides her, and not Mary. "Martha! Martha!" he says, "there is but one thing which is worth much care and thought, and that thing is Mary's choice. She longs to know me, who am the way, the truth, and the life." Not long from this time Christ took a case like this of Martha's for a text from which to preach to the train who went with him. He bade them take no thought as to what they should eat and wear. He did not mean that we should not think of these things at all, but that we should not fret our souls with care as to food and clothes, as if they were the chief end of life. God takes care of the birds which have no store house or barns in which to lay up food. God clothes the plants which do not toil or spin, with such bright hues as no king of earth can wear. If God takes such care of these birds and plants, can't you trust Him to take care of you, who are far more dear to Him? The world is full of care and fret as to its food and clothes and like things, but God wants his dear child to show forth His praise by trust in Him. Cast all your cares on Him.

We may be sure that Mary did not sit still at Christ's feet from a bad cause; from sloth or from want of love for Martha. Christ would not have said that hers was the "good part" in that case. We shall soon hear of a deed of Mary's which proves that she took great pains, and spent a large sum, to show her love for Jesus.

But first I must tell you of a dark cloud which casts its shade on this sweet home in Bethany. Lazarus falls sick. Martha and Mary think at once of Jesus in this hour of grief. But Jesus is on the shore of the Jordan, more than a score of miles from them. But they send to him at once this word: " Lord, he whom you love is sick." They did not need to tell Christ how dear Lazarus was to them, and that he was their stay and staff. Christ knew it all, and would be sure to help them they thought. But their faith is put to a hard test. Christ does not fly to them, as they thought he would. He stays still in the place where he was, two long days. At the end of that time he says to the twelve, "Let us go to Judea once more." They try to keep him from this risk of his life, for the Jews of that part of the land had tried more than once to kill him.

But Jesus said, "Our friend Lazarus sleeps, but I go that I may wake him out of sleep."

"Lord, if he sleep he shall do well." But Jesus had meant the sleep of death, and now tells them in plain words, " Lazarus is dead. And I am glad for your sakes that I was not there, that your faith may be made strong. But let us go to him." Then Thomas said to the rest of the twelve, " Let us go too, that we may die with him." They felt that the risk was great, and their wish was to share it with him. When Jesus and his friends reach Bethany they find that Lazarus is in truth dead, as he had told them, and has lain four days in the grave.

A throng of friends are with Martha and Mary in their house to weep and wail with them. But when Martha hears that Christ is near at hand, she leaves the host of friends and goes to meet the one friend whose love is worth more than all the rest. But Mary sits still in the house.

As soon as Martha caught sight of Jesus she cried out " Lord, if thou hadst been here he would not have died !" She has so much faith as that, and seems to have had still more, for she adds, " and I know that though he is now dead, yet God will give thee all things which thou wilt ask of him."

Jesus said, " Lazarus shall rise from the dead." " Yes, Lord, I know that he shall rise at the last day when all the dead shall rise." She has not yet full faith in Christ, so he tells her in plain words that it is through him that Lazarus (and all the dead) must rise from death and live once more. " He that hath faith in me though he were dead, yet shall he live, and he who lives and has faith in me shall not die. Have you this faith?" Then Martha said, "Yes, Lord; I have faith that thou art the Christ, the Son of God, which should come to this world." When she had said this she went back to the house, and told Mary (by stealth, so that the crowd who were there to wail and shriek, and make as much noise as they could, which was their way to mourn, would not hear her): "the Lord has come and calls for you." As soon as Mary heard that, she rose with haste and went to meet him. He had not yet come through the gate of the town, but was in the place where Martha had met him.

When the crowd in the house saw

Mary go out in such haste, they thought she had gone to Lazarus' grave to weep there, so they went too.

Mary greets Christ just as Martha had done, " Lord, if thou hadst been here, Lazarus would not have died." She fell at his feet and wept, and the Jews who were with her wept. and most of all, Jesus wept. It was said of him long long years ere he came to this world that he would, when he came, " bear our griefs." And this scene in Bethany is one proof of it. The sight of Christ's tears moves the hearts of the Jews who stand by, and they say, " How fond of Lazarus he was !" And some of them who had heard of, or seen some of the signs which he had wrought, said, "Could not this man who has made blind eyes see, have kept Lazarus from death?"

This was said as the whole train, and Jesus with them, were on the way to the grave; for Jesus had said, "Where have you laid him?" and they had cried "Come and see." When they reach the place, Christ bids them take off the stone from the mouth of the cave. The tombs in that land were hewn in the rocks, and a stone was made to serve as a door.

Martha thought Christ's wish must be to see the face of his dear friend once more in the flesh, and she bids him call to mind how long he has been dead, and that it will be best to think of his face as it was in health, and not look at it now that death and the grave have done their sad work.

But Jesus said to Martha, "Did I not tell you that if you would have faith you should see how God could work?"

Then those who stood by did as Christ bade them, and took off the stone from the place where the dead man was laid. Jesus gave thanks to God, and said, "I thank thee that thou hast heard me. I know that thou dost hear me at all times; but for the sake of those who stood by I said it, that they may know that thou hast sent me." Then Jesus cried with a loud voice, "Lazarus, come forth!"

How full of awe and hope must have been the eyes of Martha and

Mary as they watch the door of that tomb which for four long days and nights has hid from them their dear one, whom they thought they had seen for the last time on earth.

But there he stands in the door! Bound hand and foot, with grave clothes, to be sure, and his pale face bound with a cloth, but it is he, and he lives!

"Loose him, and let him go," said their Lord. Do you think Martha and Mary could let strange hands loose those white bands from the face and hands and feet of Lazarus? What a glad hour that must have been to them and to those who had come to mourn with them! But all were not glad. Not a few of the Jews who saw what Jesus had done had faith in him, and were his friends from that hour. But there were those there who could look on that scene with hard hearts and go off with a scowl of hate for Jesus, to plot for his death.

When the news was thus brought to the chief priests and chief sect of the Jews, that Jesus whom they had long sought to kill, had wrought such a grand sign of his might as to raise the dead, they met at once to lay plans for his death. " He does great things they said," and if we let him go on in this way he will draw all men to him and stir them up to throw off the yoke of Rome. And then Rome will come with all her hosts, and crush us."

But Caiaphas, the high priest, spoke words that meant far more than he thought of. "It is best" said he "that one should die for us, so that we may not all die,"

It was in truth best for the Jews and for us and for all the world that Christ should die, but that made the sin of those who put him to death no less. The court broke up, but not till they had sworn to put Jesus to death, and made a law that no one should know where Christ was, and not tell them, so that they might take him.

So Jesus and the twelve went to Ephraim a town of Judea, and staid there till the time for the spring feast of the Jews drew near, and then they set forth for Jerusalem. On the way a band of ten men met them. All these men had that foul plague from which no skill of man could cleanse them. They had had to fly from their homes and all their friends, and no one could bear to look at them. Christ had more than once wrought a cure on those who had the same plague. These men must have known this, for as soon as they saw him, though they stood far off, as the law bade them, yet they cried to him, "Jesus, Lord, help us!" Jesus did not touch them, he just said, "Go, show your flesh to the priests."

They had so much faith that they set out at once, though their flesh is so vile they can not bear to look at it; but as they are on the way, they are made well! Now what should you have done if such a cure as that had been wrought for you? I will tell you what one of these ten men did. When he sees that he is made well, he turns back at once, and gives praise to God with a loud voice, as he makes his way back to the feet of Jesus. And when he comes up with him he falls down on his face and gives thanks. One out of ten to say "thank you," for such a gift as that! "Were there not ten who were made clean?" asks Jesus, "but where are the nine? There is but one who comes back to give praise to God!" To the man at his feet, he said, "Rise, go thy way; thy faith hath made thee whole." The rest may have had clean flesh once more, but this one man bore off with him a clean heart too.

It was on this last trip to Jerusalem too, that Jesus spoke those dear words to those who brought their babes to him, that he might touch them. They knew that he was now to leave them, for he had told them in plain words that he was on his way to Jerusalem to die. But they long to have his hand rest on the head of each child, and no doubt think that his touch will keep them from sin and harm through life. " I wish that his hand had been laid on my head!"—the sweet song says.

But the twelve who stood with Jesus did not look on this scene as they ought. Christ had no time to waste on babes, they thought, so they bade those who had brought them there, go, and not vex the Lord with such small things. It has gone out of their minds so soon that Jesus had told them that no one could please

God till his heart was made like that of a child. But Jesus calls back those whom the twelve have sent off with sad hearts. " Let the babes come to me, for of such hearts as these is God's realm made up." Then he took them up in his arms, and put his hands on them to bless them. Christ went on his way to the cross. Life went on to these babes, till by-and-by the call came to each of them to go and live in God's House on high.

It came to some, no doubt, while they were still young, and to some not till grey hairs were to be seen in place of the soft down on which Jesus had laid his hand. But soon or late, to all of them the smiles of Jesus' face as he saw them come in, must have made them feel at once quite at home in that new world of joy. But he knows your face just as well as he did theirs, and if you love him, will greet you with the same glad smile.

As Jesus went out from the house where the babes had been brought to him, a young man came to him whom the Lord loves as soon as he sees him. He does not come by stealth, as Nicodemus did, though he too is rich and of high rank. His zeal to see Jesus is so great that he runs to meet him and kneels right in the street in the sight of all, and asks, " Good Lord, what shall I do that I may have the life that shall not end ?" Jesus said, " Thou dost know the ten laws which God gave Moses." " Oh, yes," he said, " I have kept all those from my youth." But though

Jesus loves him, yet he sees the flaw in him. "Thou dost lack one thing: go thy way, sell all that thou hast, and give to the poor, and thou shalt be an heir of God; and come take up the cross and go in my foot prints." The young man was sad at this, and left Jesus with much grief; but he left him, for he had great wealth!

He had the chance to be a prince in God's own realm and yet lost it for the sake of his piles of trash which the moths and rust could eat up, and from which death would soon cut him off.

As the train went on up to Jerusalem, Jesus went first. His friends, though they went too, yet went with fear, and strange thoughts stir their hearts. He tells the twelve once more in plain words, what will soon come to pass: "We are on our way to Jerusalem and the son of man shall be brought to the chief priests and the scribes, and they shall doom him to death, and give him up to the spears of Rome. They shall mock him, and scourge him, and shall spit on him, and kill him, and the third day he shall rise from the dead." The twelve seem to have thought that some great scene was soon to take place from these words of Christ; but they did not yet know what sort of a throne Christ's would be.

Salome the wife of Zebedee came to Jesus at this time to ask a great thing of him for her sons who came with her. This is what she begs:

"Grant that these my two sons may

sit one on the right hand and one on the left when thou art king!" "Ye know not what ye ask. Can ye drink of my cup that I shall drink of?" They said, "We can." They had no thought of what woe he was to drink, and how he must shed his blood, and when they said, "We can," they did not know that they should in truth go through pain and toil and blood to win their crowns, though Jesus gives them proof that so it shall be. "Ye shall in truth drink of my cup," he said, "but to sit on my right hand and my left is not mine to give. God knows whom that place is for." When the rest of the twelve heard what had been done by Salome, and her sons, they were vext with James and John that they had tried in this way to get the best place in the new King's Court. But Christ calls them all to him, and tries to teach them how things should be done by those who have been taught in his school. "It is the way of the world to let the great rule; but it shall not be so with you. If one wants to be great in my school, let him wait on the rest; and if one wants to be chief, let him serve the best. As the head of the school, the Son of man came not to have men serve him, but to serve them and give his life for them."

Now Christ and his band of friends come to Jericho, and there their train grew still more large, for a great throng were on their way to the feast. A blind man, Bartimæus, by name, sat by the way-side so as to have a good chance to beg of all who went by on their way to Jerusalem. But he hears on the lips of the crowd a name which drives out of the blind man's mind all thought of mere alms. When he heard that Jesus of Nazareth was near at hand, he cried, " Jesus, thou son of David, help me!" And the more those who stood near tried to stop him, the more a great deal he cried, " Thou son of David, help me!"

His voice was heard by Jesus, and he bade that the man should be brought to him. Some of his friends went to call him and said, " Be of good cheer ; rise, he calls for thee"— as if the mere call of Christ made it sure that he would give him his sight. Bartimæus when he heard this, rose and cast off his robe, so that he could make haste to Jesus. Jesus when he saw him at his feet said, " What wilt thou that I should do to thee?" The blind man cried, " Lord, that I may see!" " Go thy way; thy faith hath made thee whole." And at once sight came to his eyes. But Bartimæus did not fail to thank Jesus for what he had done. He joins his train, and as he goes, gives praise to God for what has been done to him, and all who see it give praise to God.

In the town of Jericho there dwelt a rich man, who had heard much of Jesus. He was the chief of those who took toll for Rome, and so though he had great wealth, yet the Jews bore him great ill will. But his zeal to see Jesus is so great that he runs on in front, so that he may get a good place to stand and see him pass. But he is so short that he fears he can not see well in such a crowd, so he climbs a tree by the side of the road. From his safe perch he looks down at his ease on the dense throng, and on the young Jew, on whom all eyes are bent. No such thought is in the head of Zacchæus as that Jesus will care to see him. But as the shade of the tree falls on the head of the way worn Lord, he looks up through its boughs, and sees the small man who peers down at him. He reads Zacchæus at once, as none of the proud Jews who scorn him have done. He sees the man and not his trade.

How the heart of Zacchæus must have beat as Jesus calls him by name, and says, with a smile, " Make haste and come down, for I must be thy guest to day!" He took great pains to get just a glimpse of the Lord, and now the Lord of his own free will makes choice of him to be his host! It is not strange that Zacchæus should have "made haste and come down" and have made Jesus his guest with joy. The crowd were full of spite and scorn when they saw that Jesus had made choice of such a man as his host. But their spite and scorn did Christ and Zacchæus no harm. The peace of God come to that house, and a clean heart and a new life to Zacchæus from that day. The first proof he gives of this is to stand up and say to Christ so that all who throng the house can hear the vow, " Lord, I will give the half of my goods to the poor, and to all whom I made to pay too great a tax, I will give back five times what I took." The crowd had the thought that Christ had set up high claims; that he was, in truth, on his way up to Jerusalem to seize a throne and reign as king of the Jews. "But" thought they, "if he were what he says he is, he would not be the guest of a man who, though a Jew, yet helps Rome to lay its yoke on our neck, and makes all his wealth out of what he steals from us, and the hire which Rome pays him." But you see that Christ did more than make good his claim to the name of King of the Jews, by what he did this day. He made good his claim to the name of JESUS, one who saves; and that was what no king on earth could do.

When Zacchæus has made his vow of a new life Jesus, he who saves, says to him, "This day my grace has come to you," and then he adds, for the sake of those who doubt and sneer, "he too is a child of Abraham, just as much as you are, and the Son of man has come to seek and to save that which was lost."

From Jericho Jesus goes on to Bethany. The great train which has grown more and more large all the way, makes its way on to Jerusalem, but Christ and the twelve stop at Bethany. Here is that sweet home where he has been at all times the king of guests, but now since he brought back Lazarus to life, what can they do to show how they prize him? We may be sure that they would spare no toil or pains. They all go to dine at the house of one Simon, and Martha can not sit at ease, but serves at the feast, that she may show her love for Christ.

Lazarus sits with him at the feast, and a crowd of Jews who have heard by this time that Jesus is in Bethany walk out from Jerusalem to see him and the man whom he has brought back to life. As the feast goes on Mary gives the proof which I told you she would give, that she is glad to spend a great sum to do a kind deed for Christ.

She brings a pound of the most choice balm, worth its weight in gold, and bathes with it Christ's feet, and wipes them with her own hair. Christ has been on the march now for a long time, a march which would both tire and bruise his feet. The road from Jericho to Bethany was most hard and rough, as all who have seen it say. It must have been sweet to Christ to feel the cool soft balm, but most of all, to feel what love was in the heart of her who had brought her best to him. The sweet scent fills all the house, but there is one man there whose bad heart robs the scene of all the sweet. Judas, one of the twelve, the one of whom Christ had said long since that he was a fiend, does not like what Mary has done at all. "Why was not this balm sold for a great sum, as it might have been, that the poor might have had it, in place of such a waste as this?"

This he said not from care for the

poor; but he was a thief, and had the bag in which all the funds were kept, and had the whole charge of these funds. He had put his hand in that bag more than once for his own greed, and he could not bear to see such a prize as this box of balm would have been to him lost. O, what a mean bad heart that must have been, that could grudge a gift to Jesus at such an hour as this! It is not strange that such a heart as that should know no change, but from bad to worse, though it had been with Christ so long a time.

Not a few of the Jews who came out of Jerusalem just to stare at Jesus and the man who had come forth from the tomb where he had lain four days, at his call, went back, with faith in him, to own him as their Lord. This new proof of Jesus' might was heard at once by the chief priests, who were full of plots for his death, and they make up their minds that Lazarus too must be put to death. Lazarus as he walks through the streets in life and health, and eats and drinks in their sight, gives quite too strong proof to suit them, of the fact that Jesus was he who had the keys of death.

We have now come to the last week of the life of Jesus.

April 2nd, A. D. 33, he leaves Bethany to go to the feast. The news that he is on his way spreads through the streets of Jerusalem, and a great stream of old and young pass out through the gates to meet him.

Jesus sent on two of his friends to the small town of Bethphage on the slope of the Mount of Olives, and bade them bring him a colt which they would find tied there. He told them just where they would find the ass and its colt, on which no man had as yet sat, and if some one should ask them why they took it, they were to say, " The Lord has need of him." They soon brought back the colt, and made a seat for Christ on its back, with some of their robes, and he rode thus to the great town.

The great train from Jerusalem have cut down boughs from the palm trees as they have come up the green slope of the mount, and as they meet the train from Bethany they strew these in the path of Jesus. The zeal of some is so great that they pull off their robes, and cast them down too, to make a soft path for Jesus. As they wave the boughs, and strew Jesus' way with them, they shout with glad hearts, "Save, we pray! Save now, we pray, O Lord! Praise be to him who comes in the name of the Lord!"

As the vast throng move on with shouts of praise, all at once Jerusalem comes in view from the heights. At this sight, there came to Jesus the thought of how soon the pride of Jerusalem must fall; how soon the hosts of Rome would lay siege to it, starve those who dwelt there, push down its walls and burn the grand House of God. And as Jesus looks at the fair sight, and thinks of the woe that is sure to come, He weeps and cries. " If thou hadst known at least in this thy day, the things which would give thee peace! But now they are hid from thine eyes!"

Then the train winds down the mount, and through the gates of Jerusalem, and makes a great stir through all the town. All learn that Jesus of Nazareth has come, and how he has come; but none of all who knew this, knows so well what has been said in old times of the Christ as to call to mind those words of Zechariah, " Be glad oh, Jerusalem, 'Lo, thy King comes to thee. He is just and can save ; meek of heart and rides on an ass and on a colt the foal of an ass!"

How Christ spent the rest of this day we know not. As night draws on, he goes up to God's House and looks " round on all things," and then goes back to Bethany with the twelve to spend the night. The next day he went to Jerusalem, to the House of God. Here he once more, as he had done two years back, cast out those that sold and bought there, and threw down the desks of those who made change, and the seats of them who sold doves.

The blind and the lame who were wont to sit at the door to beg, came in when they knew that Jesus was there, and he made them well. Then the boys and girls who were in God's House and saw what Jesus had done, took up the glad shout, " Save, we pray, thou Son of David!"

All this, you may be sure, made

the chief priests and scribes still more mad with rage.

The next day when Jesus taught in the house of God, they came to him to know who gave him the right to teach and work such signs as he had done. He bids them first tell him one thing, "Was John the Baptist sent from God, or was he of men?" They dare not say yes or no to this. If they said John came from God, then Christ would of course say, why did you not take his word then when he said of me, "This is the Lamb of God, who bears the sins of the world," "This is the Son of God?" And they dare not say he came from men, for all who were there with them had faith in John as sent by God.

And then Jesus told them one of those tales of his, which means far more than it seems to mean at first. Once there was a man who set out vines, and put a hedge round them, and dug a place for the wine press and built a lodge, and then let out the grounds to those who were to take care of them, and went to a far off land.

When the time came for the grapes to be ripe the lord sent a man to these grounds of his to get the fruit. But those who had the charge of the grounds caught the man and beat him, and sent him off with no fruit at all. Then the Lord sent a new man to them, and at him they threw stones, and gave him wounds in the head, and much ill use. One by one the Lord sent a host of men to get what was his due from these grounds, but those who were in charge slew some of them, and beat the rest.

Now the Lord had still left his one son, most dear to him. So last of all, he sent his son to them, for he thought they would stand in awe of his son. But when he came to them, they said, "This is the heir: come, let us kill him, and the grounds will be ours." So they took him and slew him, and cast him out of that which was his own. Now what will the Lord of that vine yard do?"

Those who heard Christ speak said, "Why he will crush, and make an end of these bad men, and will let out his vine yard to those who will give him its fruit." They knew right well what this tale meant, and that they were the bad men who kept back the fruit from God, who now had sent his Son to them, whom they sought to slay. But they did not want to seem to those who stood by, to be hit by it, and so they spoke in such a prompt way of what the doom of the men should be.

Christ does not let them off in this way. He tells them in plain words that he means them and no one else. " I say to you that God shall take from you what he has let you hold in trust for him, and will give it to those who will give its fruits to him."

This made them hate Jesus all the more, but they dare not lay hands on him then, for they knew that all who stood by had faith in him. But they set sharp men to watch him, that they might catch him in his words. The first set whom they sent, came with a lie in their mouths. "Lord, we know that thou art true, and dost teach the way of God in truth, and hast no fear of man at all. Now we want to know what thou dost think. Is it right for us Jews who are God's own heirs to pay a tax to Cæsar, and thus own that we are the slaves of Rome?" But Jesus saw their bad hearts, and the trap which they had set for him, and said, "Why do you tempt me, you cheats! Show me some of the coin with which you pay the tax." So, they brought him one of their pence. "Whose face is this on this coin and whose seal?" "Cæsar's." "Then give to Cæsar the things which are Cæsar's, and give to God the things which are God's." They were caught in their own trap, and went their way in shame.

New men took their place, and sought to catch Christ in like ways, but they all were put to shame by him.

At last Jesus turns on those who thus plot for his death, and reads out to them woe on woe which shall be their doom, for their life of cheats and shams. They took such care to seem good in the eyes of men that they did not care at all that their hearts were foul in the sight of God. But Christ rends off the veil from their hearts, and shows them just how mean and vile they are, and tells them that God's curse is on them now, and shall not pass from them.

These dread words end in a sad wail, wrung from the heart of Christ at the thought of what the fate of Jerusalem must be. O Jerusalem! Jerusalem! how have I sought to save you from your fate, and shield you from your foes, as a hen doth shield her brood with her wings, but you would not come to me! and now it is too late!"

When Jesus and his friends went out that night from God's house one of them bade Christ look at the stones of which it was built, and see how grand and fine the whole rich pile was. But Christ said, "I tell you the days will come in which all these stones shall be thrown down."

And so it came to pass in two score years, and some of them would live to see that sad hour. Christ had stood in that house of God for the last time. They all went out, as was their wont, to Bethany to lodge there. But as they sat down to rest on the slope of the Mount of Olives, Jesus spoke to them of what their own fate should be, and how much they would have to bear for his name's sake. He told them, too, once more, of the doom which was to come on fair Jerusalem, which with all its pride lay spread at their feet as they sat there. And last of all, he told them of how the world should come to an end, and bade them watch and pray, lest the world should end for them at an hour when they were not fit to meet the Son of man. He bade them use all their skill and strength to take care of his

MOUNT OLIVET.

work which he must so soon leave in their hands. Then to cheer them, he tells them that in the great last day, when God will judge all the world, he will count all that has been done to them and to all who love him, as if it had been done to him.

On Wednesday, April 5th A.D. 33, Christ seems to have spent the day in Bethany, or on the Mount of Olives. His work in Jerusalem was done. But one of the twelve, one of that band of most dear friends whose life had been one with his for the past three years, had much work to do in town that day. Judas had had up to this time hopes that Jesus would prove to be the Christ; that he would put to shame all his foes, and raise all his friends to great rank in his new realm.

But he sees now that Jesus does not mean to do this. So he thinks he he will make as much as he can out of Christ. He knows how the high court plot for the death of his Lord, and how glad they would be to get hold of him by stealth, so as not to raise the rage of the crowds who had come up from Galilee and all parts of the land where Jesus had taught and wrought cures.

Judas has heard that the court sits that day in the house of the high priest, and he makes up his mind to go and see what they will pay him to show them how they can take Jesus with guile. They are right glad to see the false man come in; and pledge him the price for which a slave could be bought in those days—$21. But bad as they were, what scorn they must have felt for the mean wretch who could thus sell his friend!

From that hour Judas sought a chance to give up Jesus to the court in such a time and way as not to rouse the rage of his friends.

The next day was that on which the great feast was to be kept, when the lamb was to be slain at God's house, and all were to eat of it, and think of how God had freed them from the hand of Pharaoh. The twelve went to ask Jesus where it was his wish that they should eat the feast. He bade them go to town, and told them they would meet a man in the street with a jar (which he may have just been to fill at the well). They were to track him home, and when he should stop at a house, they were to go in and say to the good man of that house, "The Lord bids us say to thee, 'My time is at hand. I will keep the feast at thy house with my friends?' He will show you a large guest room in which you may set out the feast."

This was done, and as night drew on Jesus left Bethany and went to Jerusalem to the house where they were to meet. When it was time for them to take their seats at the feast, what do you think the twelve fall to a strife for? Why they all want the best seat!

Jesus chides them for this more by his acts than by his words. He rose from his seat, laid off his loose robe, and did for them all that which some of them should have done for him.

His walk from Bethany through the dust made the foot bath, which is the first thing with which one serves his guests in that land, a great need. But none of them all thought to do this kind thing for their Lord. They were full of thoughts of self, though Jesus had told them long since that that was not to be the way of those who would please him. That in his realm, he was to count as chief who could serve best. Christ must have brought all these things back to their minds, as he, though he come from God and was so soon to go back to God, went from place to place and bent down to bathe the feet of each of the twelve! What shame they must have felt for their strife as to which should have the best place, when they saw their Lord stoop down and do such an act for them!

When Christ came to Peter he cried, "Lord thou shalt not wash my feet!" But Jesus said, "If I wash thee not thou hast no part with me." And then Peter begs that Christ will wash his hands and his head, as well as his feet. "He that is clean needs but to wash his feet; and ye are clean, but not all" said Christ; and he meant by this, that he could see Judas' foul heart.

When Christ had gone back to his seat, he told the twelve why he had done this for them: "Ye call me Lord, and ye do well, for so I am. If I, then, your Lord, wash your feet, you ought to do the same." "You need not think that it is too great a task for you to do what you have seen your Lord do."

Now in our day, and in our land it would be a mere form to wash the feet as Jesus did. The shoes which were worn, when he was on earth, were not at all like ours. Men did not wear hose, and the shoes were mere soles with straps to hold them on the foot. Of course a short walk through the dust would soil the foot. The way was to leave your shoes at the door when you went to make a call or to dine, and sit with bare feet, and a slave would bathe them for you as soon as you went in. That is not our way, so Jesus could not have meant that we must do just that one act if we would be like him. Did he not mean that we should think no act too small or low for us to do, if by it we can make some one else feel more at ease?

Then the feast went on much as it had done at that time when Jesus had come up to Jeruselam to keep it when he was twelve years old. But in the midst of the feast the heart of Jesus was wrung by the thought, that small as was this band of friends who sat with him at that feast, they were not all true to him. There sat Judas, and ate and drank with them as if he were one of them, but his heart was not there, and his head was full of plots as to how he could best do what he had sworn to do. How could he give up Jesus who sat there and said to the twelve, "My heart's wish has been to keep this feast with you?" How could he give Jesus up to the chief priests with the least noise, and clutch the price of his blood! How would he spend it when he had got it?—for it was a large sum to him. Jesus may have seen the scowl which these thoughts brought to the face of Judas, for we read that his soul was sad, and he said, "One of you who sits with me here shall give me up to death! His hand is now on the board with me!" Judas' heart must have stood still for a few beats at these words. What if the game were all lost, and Christ who knew his heart so well, were to strike him dead with a word, or to tell the rest of the band what was his plan, and they should set on him and kill him, and he should so lose the prize, and his life too?

But Christ speaks once more, and Judas sees that he does not mean to stop him in his base course by such means. The Son of man must die, for that is the one way by which he can win life for the world;—but woe to that man by whose means this shall come to pass!"

Then all the twelve cried one by one, "Lord, is it I?" None of them seems to have thought of Judas as more apt to do this base deed than was he, and the shock of Christ's sad words is so great that no one knows what to think, and each doubts his own heart. "Lord, is it I!" And Christ said to them, "It is one of the twelve which shall dip with me in the dish." This did not lay their fears to rest, so Peter made a sign to John (who sat next to

Jesus and laid his head on his breast) to ask him once more to tell whom he meant. So John asks, "Lord, who is it?" But Jesus says much as he had done at first, "It is he to whom I shall give a sop when I dip it." One dish which they had at this feast was a sauce made of sour wine and dates and figs. When the time came to serve the herbs (like our cress, it may be), which were part of the feast, the chief would wrap them round a piece of bread and dip them in this sauce and pass them on to each of the guests. So Jesus did at this time, and Judas seems to have been the first to whom he gave this "sop." Judas seems to have sat near Jesus, where he could hear his low voice as he spoke to John. When he took the sop he was so false as to ask, "Lord, is it I?" Then said Jesus to him, "Thou hast said," and then adds, "What you mean to do, do with speed."

Some of those that heard these words thought Jesus meant that Judas, who kept all their funds, should go out and give alms to the poor, so they let him pass out, and Christ was left with none but true friends with him. Then with what words of love does Jesus speak to them! You can find no words half so sweet, and yet so full of strength and cheer in all the books of the world. You must learn them all by heart, for he meant them for you as well as for John and Peter, and the rest of those who sat there with him that night. You can find them in St. John's life of Christ.

But in the midst of those good bye words, Jesus turns to Peter, and warns him to take care of his faith lest it should fail when it meets the first shock. Simon! Simon! Satan wants you, that he may sift you like wheat; but I pray for you that your faith may not fail. And when you have got up from your fall you will know how to hold up those who are weak." Peter could not bear the thought that he should not stand firm, and cried out, " Lord! I will go with thee to death!" "I tell thee, Peter, the cock shall not crow this day ere thou shalt have said three times thou dost not know me!"

While they still sat at the board, Jesus told his friends what he would like to have them do from time to time to keep him in mind when he should have gone back to his home on high. It is such a small thing that it can be done by the poor quite as well as by the rich, and it seems as if there were no time or place where it can not be done, if one loves Jesus and wants to please him.

This is what he would have them do. He took one of the thin cakes of bread which were made use of at the feast, and broke it in bits, and gave it to them and said, " Take, eat, this is my flesh which I give for you. Do this that you may keep me in mind"— me, my words, my deeds.

Then he took the wine cup which made part of the feast, and gave thanks, and gave it to them with the words, " Drink ye all of it. This is my blood, which is shed to wash out your sins."

And so to this day, we do as he bade his friends do that night. We keep a feast from time to time, in which we eat bread, and drink from a cup, and think of Jesus, and what he did for us. Each time we do so, Jesus gives us a new pledge of his love to us, which was so great that he laid down his own life for us, and we give him a pledge that we will love and serve him. St. Paul says, "As oft as ye eat this bread and drink of this cup, ye do show forth the Lord's death till he come."

Jesus spoke more words of peace and love to them, and then they hear him pray more for them than for his own sake, though pain, and the cross, and death are, as he knows, so near him. Then they sung a hymn, (the words were no doubt those of one or more of the last six Psalms of David), and went out, though it was night, to the Mount of Olives. Here was a grove of the trees which gave their name to the mount, where he had been wont to go to seek rest, and to pray. When they came to the gate which led to this nook, he took Peter and James and John in with him, but bade the eight "Sit ye here while I go and pray."

What Jesus went through that night in that grove I shall not try to tell you. It was such woe as you and I can not weigh. It was so great as to crush the Son of God to the earth, and make him sweat great drops of blood, though he knelt there in the cool of the night, and cry to God to

CHRIST'S AGONY IN THE GARDEN.

let the cup pass from him if that could be his will. That it was woe so great that none like it has been or can be known on earth, we know, but just what it was, God knows and not man.

And through it all Jesus' best friends slept!

Three times he kneels and prays, and three times he goes back to the three whom he had bade to watch with him, and pray. Each time he finds them in a deep sleep, and with no words of strength and cheer and love for him in that hour when their sins, and the sins of the world, wrung his heart. The last time he came back to them he woke them with the cry, " Do you sleep now, and take your rest? The hour is come. Lo he who will give me up to death is at hand." The ear of Jesus has caught a sound which those who were left at the gate have not yet heard. It is the tramp of a band of men which he hears, and soon the gleam of torch lights is seen, and the flash of arms. In the rear of this band comes a great crowd with swords and staves, and in front comes the well known form of Judas!

This is the last time when the twelve will all meet on earth. And their Lord is with them, as he has been through the past three years, but what a scene was this last which they were to pass through! Judas greets Jesus with a kiss. He has been wont to do this no doubt, for in the east that is the way men meet their friends.

But the kiss of to night is a sign. Judas had told the band, "He whom I shall kiss, that same is he! Take him, hold him fast, and lead him back to those who sent you." The eyes of Judas can not have met the eyes of Jesus at this time! How could he look him in the face?

"Hail, Lord!" said he, as he gave him the false kiss.

"Friend, (how that word 'friend' must have stung him!) why art thou come? Judas, dost thou give up the Son of man to death with a kiss?"

That is all which he has to say to Judas.

Then Jesus steps forth from the shade of the grove to meet the band, and asks, "Whom seek ye?" "Jesus of Nazareth." "I am he." At these words they shrank back, and fell to the ground. One word from him and they would all have been dead men; but he would not speak that word. His hour had come. He lets them rise, and asks once more, "Whom seek ye?" And they said, "Jesus of Nazareth." " Have I not told you I am he? If ye seek me, take me, and let these men who are with me go their way."

When Jesus' friends saw the band lay hold of him and bind his hands, they said, " Lord, shall we not smite with the sword?" And Peter, who could not wait to be told, smote with such haste that he did not take good aim, and just cut off the ear of one of the men!"

With what grace Christ speaks

then to this rude mob which has bound him: " Let me do this much!" and then he heals the man's ear with a touch, and bids Peter sheath his sword with words like these. " Do you think that this mob could take me, if I did not let them? If I would but ask for them, would not God send his hosts to my aid? But how then could that end for which I came to the world be brought to pass?" To the chief priests, and to all the crowd which came out to seize him he said, " Why have you come out to take me as if I were a thief, with swords and staves? I sat with you in God's house, and taught you from day to day, but you laid no hands on me. But this is your hour." When Jesus' friends heard these words from him, they knew that there was no hope that he would use his might to save his own life; so they all left him and fled! All but Judas, who goes with the band that he may clutch the price of Jesus' blood.

Jesus was led at once to the house of the high priest, where were all the chief priests and the whole court, though it was not yet dawn. They dare not wait till day, but make haste to do their foul work and doom Jesus to death, by stealth, so that his friends may not try to save him.

Peter soon made his way to the high priest's house, and there he met John, who was known to the high priest, and so he could go in and take his friend in as well. It was cold, so the guards made a fire in the hall or court and Peter sat down with them to get warm, and " to see the end." All this time Jesus stood with bound hands, and no one, of all the scores on scores whom he had blest with sight and health and life, to speak a word for him to that court of proud hard men.

Though Peter was not in the same room with Jesus, yet he would hear much that went on, through the guards who went and came. He was so ill at ease that the sharp eyes of the maid who kept the door were drawn to him, and she soon said, " This man was with him who is now at the bar of the court :—are you not one of that man's friends ?" And what did the brave Peter say to this ; he who had told Jesus two or three hours since that he would die with him ? He did just what Jesus had told him he would do ; he said, " I do not know what you mean ; I do not know the man!" But he takes fright at the words and keen eyes of the maid, and leaves the warm fire, and goes out to the porch. There a man soon marks his wan, down cast face, and sees at once, that he does not lounge there as the rest do, with not much care as to how the case comes out. Peter's eyes are full of fear and care, and the man says, " Thou, too, art one of them !" And Peter says " Man, I am not!"

It seems as if he must have tried to seem at his ease, and talk of what had come to pass as if he were one of the band who had brought in Jesus. At least, we know that he spoke too much for his own good. The brogue of

Galilee was a strong one. Most, if not all, who stood at the porch, or by the fire in the hall were from Judea. When they heard Peter's brogue, more than one of them said; " Why, you must be one of them! You are from Galilee; your speech proves it." Then did Peter curse and swear, " I know not the man of whom you speak!" Where the Lord stood we know not, but it was not so far from Peter (though not in the same room) but that he could hear all his words, and see him if he would turn his head.

As Jesus stands face to face with the court who will soon doom him to death, he hears this third " I know not the man," from his friend who has sworn to stand by him to the last. And Jesus and Peter both hear the crow of a cock that hails the dawn. " Then did the Lord turn and look on Peter!" If Peter had not been at heart a true good man, then that look from Jesus would have sent him out to make way with his own life.

All came to mind. It was just as Jesus had said, " Ere the cock shall crow, thou shalt thrice say, I know him not!" But he was a good man, though not so strong and true as he had thought he was, and that look from Christ sent him out to weep tears of shame and grief, and live a brave, true life. And in the end his rash words came true; he did go through all things for the sake of Christ, and die for him on a cross like his own!

The court could make out no case. When they ask Jesus to tell the names

PETER'S DENIAL OF CHRIST.

of those who were in his school, and to make known what he has taught, Jesus bids them not ask him, but ask the crowds whom he has taught from church to church, in all the land, and in the House of God at Jerusalem, One of the guards who stood by struck Jesus, (his hands were bound fast you know) with the palm of his hand, and said, " Dost thou speak in that way to the high priest?" " If I speak ill, prove it; but if well, why dost thou smite me?" said Jesus. No proofs could be brought that he had done or said aught that was bad. But at last, two false men were brought in who swore that they had heard him say that he could tear down the House of God, and build it up in three days. When the high priest bade him make known what he had to say to this charge, Jesus held his peace.

Then the high priest said to him, "Art thou the Christ the Son of God? I charge thee in the name of God to tell us if thou be the Christ, the Son of God." Jesus saith, "I am; But ye shall yet see the Son of man sit on the right hand of God, and come in the clouds."

Then the high priest rent his clothes, to show what a shock it gave him to hear Jesus thus claim to be the Son of God. "What need have we to seek for proofs? We have heard his own words. What do you think?" Then all the court said, "He ought to be put to death."

The court broke up now for a time,

to meet once more in a few hours. Jesus is left in charge of the guard, in the high priest's house. Then the men that hold Jesus, mock him and smite him. Some spit on him. Then they blind his eyes and strike him in the face, and bid him tell who smote him. "Tell us, thou Christ, who is he who smote thee." Jesus, faint with the woe which he had borne in Gethsemane, and with all that he has been through in this long night, bears all this mean spite, and ill use. He is dumb, though a word from him could have slain them all. All this took place at night, but by their laws a man could not be tried for his life at night, so the court had to meet once more by day, to make sure what they had done.

As soon as it was day Jesus was led to the court, and the same form was gone through with as when they had sat at night. They ask, "Art thou the Christ?" and he says, "If I tell you, you will not have faith in me." Then said they all: "Art thou then the Son of God?" He said to them "Ye say that I am." Then they all said, "What need have we to hear proof? We have heard it from his own mouth."

There was one man to whom the doom of Christ by the court brought grief, and shame, and death. Things had not come out at all as Judas had thought they would. It was plain that Jesus would not use his might to save his own life, nor prove that he was the Christ of God by some great sign, which should force the court to own him.

Then there was Judas' own case. He was, of course, cast out by his old friends who were of Jesus' school, but no one else took him up! The chief priests and scribes who had made him their tool have no word for him now they have got Jesus in their hands. They pay him his bribe, but bad as they are, they scorn him as he takes it, for it is, at least, the price of the blood of his best friend, and much as they want men who will swear in their court that Jesus has said such and such words, they tempt Judas with no more bribes. He was then, as now, and through all time he will be, the scorn of the foes as well as of the friends of Christ.

His poor soul can bear no more.

He breaks in on the court which would not call him, and at this late hour gives in his word for Jesus. His is the first voice to speak for him, in whom was no sin. He cries, " It is my sin that I gave up to you him who is pure of all sin!" With cool scorn the court say, " What is that to us? see thou to that." Then Judas cast down the bribe for which he had sold the blood of his Lord and his own soul, and went out and put an end to his own life.

The chief priests pick up the coin, but will not put it back with the funds of the house of God, for it has the stain of blood on it, since it bought the blood of Jesus.

With some talk as to how it is best to spend it, they at last make up their minds to buy a field in which to lay the dead who have no tomb of their own, nor friends to give them a grave. And to this day that place which they thus bought, bears the name of Field of Blood.

Though the doom of death has been set on Christ by the court, yet they have no right to do the deed. You know the Jews were not free at this time, and they must ask leave of Rome ere they can put a man to death.

So they all rose and bound Jesus, and led him to Pontius Pilate. The chief priests lead the train, and a mob join it as they go on. The priests are too pure to pass the door of Pilate's house. The next day would be God's day, and they could not keep the feast of that day if they had put their foot on the floor of a Gentile. Pilate hears the crowd at the door, and when the chief priests send for him to come out to them, he goes that he may still the mob at once ere it grow too strong for him. There they stand with a pale meek man, still young, in their midst.

What they hope is, that Pilate will bid them go and do their will with Jesus. They know that the case is too weak to bear sharp search from his eye. But Pilate does not love the Jews much, and he will not be a mere tool in the hands of their priests. He bids them tell him with what they charge the man whom they have there bound. No doubt he knew who Jesus was, for a band of his men of arms had gone out to help to bring him in from Gethsemane, and he had made too much stir in Jerusalem not to have been a man of mark to such a shrewd man as Pilate.

But the chief priests do not wish to tell Pilate how slight their charge is, so they say, "If he had not done wrong we should not have brought him to you."

Pilate says, "Take him and judge him by your law." He seems to say this to vex them, for as they now have to say the law will not let them put a man to death. Then they see that they must take a new course if they would get Pilate on their side. So they make up a fresh charge. They say, "We found this man had tried to lead the Jews to cast off the yoke of Rome. He told them not to pay

Cæsar's tax, but said he was Christ the King of the Jews.

Then Pilate took Jesus one side to talk with Him. He asks Him, "Art Thou the King of the Jews?" Jesus said, "I am; but my realm is not of this world. If it were of this world, then would they who serve me fight, and save me out of the hands of the Jews. As thou hast said, I am a king. To this end was I born, and for this cause came I to the world that I might make known the truth. He that is of the truth will hear my voice."

Pilate said to Him, "What is truth?" and then took Jesus out to the Jews, and said, "I find no fault in this man at all." Then the chief priests make up new things to say of Jesus. Pilate, as he heard them, said to Jesus,

"Dost Thou not hear all these things with which they charge Thee?" But Jesus said not a word. Then Pilate cried once more to Him, "Why dost Thou not speak when they charge Thee with such things?" But still the lips of Jesus did not move.

Then the chief priests were the more fierce, and said, "He stirs up the Jews. He has taught through all the land from Galilee to this place."

When Pilate heard that Jesus came from Galilee, he was glad of the chance to get rid of the mob and their suit. Herod, the King of Galilee, was in town at the time, so Pilate bade the chief priests take Jesus to him.

As I have told you, Herod had a strong wish to see Jesus. He had thought at one time that He must be

John the Baptist, whom he had slain, and who had come back to life.

So Herod was right glad when at last Jesus, of whom he had heard so much, was brought to him. His hope was that Jesus would do some great sign in his sight. But Jesus stood still, with meek, pale face, and bound hands. When Herod tries to rouse Him to show his might, and asks Him this and that, no words can he draw from Him. His ears seem not to hear the voice of Herod, or the base lies and fierce threats of the chief priests as they tell their tales to Herod.

Pilate and Herod had been at strife for some time, but this act of Pilate in which he sent Jesus to Herod to have him judge His case, made them good friends once more. But when Herod found that Jesus could not be made to show off his might just to make a man—king or no king—stare, it did not please Him. So Herod with his men of war set Jesus at nought, and did mock Him. They put on Him a gay robe, it may be one which Herod had cast off, and thus clad, sent Him back to Pilate.

When Pilate finds that the case yet rests with him, he still means to set Jesus free. He tells the chief priests and the mob, "I have found no fault in Jesus, nor has Herod. So I will scourge Him and then let Him go." He thought he could keep the peace with the chief priests if he should scourge Jesus, and yet he could save His life.

At each one of these feasts of the

Jews, some one who had been shut up in goal for crime was set free, and Pilate meant to let Jesus go on this plea. While he sat on the throne of the judge, his wife sent word to him that she had had a dream as to " that just man" Jesus, which gave her great fright and pain, and she bade Pilate do Him no harm.

This made Pilate's wish still more strong to set Jesus free. Once, twice, three times he tries to save him. But the mob, (some of whom had cried but a few hours since, " Save, Lord, we pray!" as Jesus rode through the gate of Jerusalem,) cried, " Not this man, but Barabbas!"

Now this Barabbas had in truth done just those things which the chief priests had said Christ had done. He had tried to stir up the Jews to throw off the yoke of Rome. More than this, he was a thief, and had shed blood.

Pilate still strove for Jesus. He asks, " But what shall I do with Jesus whom ye call the King of the Jews?" And the chief priests urge them on, and all cry out, " To the cross, to the cross with Him!" But Pilate still pleads with them, " Why, what wrong thing has He done?" But their cries ring out more loud and fierce, " To the cross with Him! to the cross with Him!" When Pilate saw how fierce the mob were, he gave in to them, and plead no more for Him who, as he said, had done no wrong.

But he stood up in the sight of all the crowd to wash his hands, as a sign that the guilt of Christ's blood would not rest on him. " I am clean of the blood of this just man," said he, "see ye to it." But the stain could not so be thrown off from his soul. Pilate could set Jesus free in spite of the chief priests and the mob. But he fears them; they might tell tales of him to great Cæsar at Rome which would cost him his place, and that, he thinks, he can not bear to lose for the sake of one man, though just and pure as Jesus.

But as Pilate stands there and makes this sign, as if he would rub off all the guilt of Jesus' death, the mob send up the mad cry, which makes our blood run cold as we think what it meant: " Let his blood be on us and on our seed!"

Then Pilate freed Barabbas, but took Jesus and gave him up to those men whose place it was to use the scourge.

I dare not think what pain the blows of those strong, rough men must have cost the weak flesh of our dear Lord. But no cry burst from his lips. It all came to pass just as Isaiah long, long years back had sung of the Christ who was to come: "I gave my back to them that smote me, and my cheek to them that pluck off the hair; I hid not my face from shame, and them that did spit on me."

When the scourge had done its work, Pilate gave Jesus up to the mob to do their will with him. His own men of war seize the chance of rare sport, as they think it, brutes that they are. The whole band pour in to join in this vile sport.

They once more put on him the red robe which Herod gave him in scorn, and which had been stript off when he gave his back to the scourge. They weave a crown for him out of a shrub which has leaves of rich dark green, but which has stiff, sharp thorns which pierce the skin as they force it on his brow. They put a reed in his right hand. They bow the knee to him and mock him as they cry, " Hail, King of the Jews!"

But they soon tire of this play, it is not so rough as they like. Then they smite him with their hands; they spit on him; they snatch from him the reed, and smite him on the head with it, though each blow drives in the thorns more and more.

Pilate, though he has made his hands clean, as he thinks, is not at ease. He hears the shouts and howls and blows of the brutes in the hall, and goes out once more to see the "just man" Jesus, whom his own act has made their prey.

The sight of the white, sad face with blood drops on the brow, but with firm sweet lips which will not curse or cry, moves the heart of Pilate. He hopes the same sight may move the mob who wait at the door, and in the street, for their turn at the grim sport. So he leads Jesus forth, in robe and crown, and pleads : " See the man! I bring him forth that you may know that I find no fault with him!"

The sight, so full of woe, seems but to rouse more thirst for the blood of Jesus, and the chief priests once more lead the cry, " To the cross with him! To the cross with him!"

But Pilate said, " You must do it, then, for I find no fault in him."

Then said the Jews, " We have a law by which he ought to die, for he says he is the Son of God."

This moves Pilate in a way they had not thought of. The fears which his wife's strange dream had brought to him, all come back. What if Jesus should be the Son of God, more strong than Cæsar, who rules the world?

He takes Jesus one side and asks him, " Whence art thou?" But Jesus does not speak.

" Wilt thou not speak to me? Dost

thou not know that I can send thee to the cross, or set thee free?"

Then at last Jesus speaks, "It is not thou, but one who has more might than thou; so the sin of him who gave me to thee is the worse."

This makes Pilate seek still more to save Jesus. He does all but the one thing which he might and should have done. If he would but call out his men of arms and show the flag of Rome, the chief priests would slink back to their homes, and the mob would melt.

But Pilate has so much sense of right and wrong as to be ill at ease, but not so much as to be brave to do right at all risks.

So when he hears the Jews (who are so sharp as to read his weak fears) cry, "If thou let this man go thou art not Cæsar's friend," he does not put them off more. He must make an end of this scene. He sits down on the throne of the judge, and once more says, "See your king!"

But they cry out, "To the cross with him!"

"Shall I send your king to the cross?" asks Pilate.

The chief priests say, "We have no king but Cæsar!"

Pilate sees the threat which lurks in their words, and yields to it. He gives up Jesus to them to be put to death on the cross.

Then the Jews take Jesus and lead him out. They, too, mock him as Pilate's men of war had done, and when they tire of this, they take off from him the king's robe, and put his own clothes on him, and lead him out through one of the gates of the town.

On his back, sore with the wounds which the scourge has made, they lay the cross of wood on which he is to die. But he is too faint and weak, from his long fast and the loss of blood, to bear it, and he sinks with its weight. They chance to meet a man whose name is Simon, who is on his way to town, and stop him, and make him bear the cross for Jesus.

Then the train once more moves on. More and more join it. There are some whose hearts ache at the sight of such shame and woe as are put on Jesus, and they break out in sobs and cries. The sad wail comes to the ears of him for whom they mourn, and he turns to speak to them: "Weep not for me, ye wives of Jerusalem! but weep for your own fate and that of those whom you have borne. The days are near at hand when she who has borne no child shall be thought the most rich of you all. Then shall all cry to the rocks, 'Fall on us!' and to the hills, 'Hide us!' for if they do these things in a green tree, what shall be done in the dry?"

This was the last time they would hear Jesus preach, and his words must have rung in the ears of some of them till the black hour of the siege came, and they and their sons were slain by the sword or died for want of food.

The place where the cross was to be set up was a round knoll, which had so much of the shape of a skull as to go by that name—THE PLACE OF A SKULL.

To add to the shame of the scene, two thieves had been brought with them to meet the same death with him who had no sin!

I could tell you a sad tale of the pain of this mode of death, but I can not bear to do so. All you need to know is, that it was as full of woe as death could be, and that Jesus bore it all for us. His love for us was so great that he gave up his life for us, so that we might be freed from sin, and share his joy on high. And he could pray for those who drove the nails, and say, " Blot out their sin, for they know not what they do."

Some one who stood by at that

hour, ere the cross to which he was held fast by nails was set up in its place, brought Jesus a draught of wine in which myrrh had been put. This was meant to dull his sense of the sharp pain, and so Christ would not drink it.

His foes did not take his life from him while he slept, or while he knew not what they did, through the drugs they gave him. He gave up his own life for us.

And now they lift up the three, and make each cross firm in its place. Jesus is in the midst, and the two thieves on the right hand and the left.

Pilate had sent a scroll to be put up on the top of Jesus' cross. He wrote it with his own hand in three tongues, so that all who went by could read it: "JESUS OF NAZARETH, THE KING OF THE JEWS."

It did not please the chief priests, as Pilate knew it would not, and they beg him to change it, at least so that it will read, " He said, I am King of the Jews."

But Pilate said, "What I wrote, I wrote," and they dare not urge him more to change it, lest they should vex him, so that he would yet save Jesus from them.

When the guard had done their work, and set up the cross, they took the spoil which fell to them. The long, full cloak which Jesus had worn they tore in four parts, one for each of them. But his "coat," the robe worn next the skin, was so wrought that it had no seam. They do not like to spoil this, so they cast lots for it, whose it shall be. When this is done, they sit down to watch there. Some of the chief men of the Jews are there to watch him, too, and they mock him with the cry, "Let him save his own life if he be the Christ of God!"

This stirs up the guard once more, and they bring Jesus sour wine to drink, but mock him as they come: "If thou be the King of the Jews, save thy own life!" This must have made the Jews wince, since their lives were not in their own hands, for they were the slaves of Rome.

The cross stood not far from the gate of the town, which was now more than full of the great crowd who came up from all parts of the land to keep the Feast, so that a throng went back and forth by the cross. All, as they draw near and read the scroll which is on Jesus' cross, feel the scorn which Pilate has shown them in its words, and vent on Jesus the rage which they dare not show to Pilate.

So they, too, wag their heads and rail on Jesus, and take up the cry of the chief priests, "If thou be the Son of God, come down from the cross, that we may see and have faith in thee!"

And the chief priests and scribes once more mock him, and cry, "He came to save us, but he can not save his own life!" They spoke the truth, though they did not mean it for truth.

To win life for the world, Jesus Christ had to give up his own life. It was true he could not, for he would not, save his own life. One poor wretch, though death stares him in the face as he hangs on the cross at Jesus' side, adds his voice to the shout of scorn and rage, and rails at him whom he must one day meet as his judge. "If thou be the Christ save thine own self and us!" But his mate, the thief who hangs on the third cross, chides him for his words; " Dost thou not fear God, since the same doom is on thee? And we in truth, ought to be here, since we have brought this doom on us by our deeds; but this man hath done no wrong.

And now Jesus, though he hangs there on the cross in the pangs of death, and seems to the eyes which glare at him in rage and scorn to drink the last dregs of loss and shame, yet does a deed more great than to have made a world. He saves a soul from death! He plants in the breast of that poor thief at his side, faith in him! What an hour was that for faith in Jesus to spring up!

His best friends had fled in grief and fear, or wept at the foot of his cross, as if his cause were lost by his death, though he had told them that just these things must come to pass. But here hangs a poor thief, who has not seen Jesus heal the sick, or cast out fiends, or raise the dead. He has not heard him preach. But he has seen how pure Jesus is, how meek he is, yes, and how strong he is, though his frail flesh is torn and sinks to death. At that dark hour, when to man's eye

Jesus has least might to bless and save, this man, with a faith born of God, trusts in him.

Did Jesus look like a king to the rest of the great throng who saw him that day, as he hung on that cross with nails through his hands and feet, and blood drops on his brow? And yet this thief who sees him now for the first time, sees the king in him! He begs Jesus to think of him when he shall come to his throne.

What a step from that cross of shame and death to the Crown of the King of Saints!

But the thief-had faith so strong that he could see Jesus as he would soon sit at the right hand of God.

I have said too much of this, it may be, but it seems to me that such great faith as this has not been known on earth. And so it came to pass in his case, as Jesus had once said to a man who came to him for aid, "As is your faith so be it to you." His Lord said to him, "I say to thee, this day thou shalt be with me in Paradise!"

"And I, if they lift me up, will draw all men to me." So Jesus had said months since, and now this thief at the point of death, leads the great host who have been drawn, and shall yet be drawn, to the cross of Jesus.

There is a group at the foot of the cross on which Jesus looks with love. In that hour of pain and death he goes on with the same work in which he has spent his life. He can think of those who are sad and in want, and bless them.

Jesus, though the Son of God, was the Son of Mary too; and there stands Mary, thrust through with the sword which old Simeon had told her should one day pierce her heart!

There too stands John who was dear to Jesus, and lay with his head on His breast at the feast on the last night. As He looks on the dear face which has been bent on him with love and awe, from the first hour of his life till now, he longs to make sure that she will have love and care to the last, and he bids John who knows most of him and his love, take his place, and be a son to her. From that hour he took her to his own home. Some have thought that as we do not hear of Mary as with her Son when his friends laid him in the tomb, Jesus meant to spare her the last pangs of his death, and so bade John take her right to the house which he made his home while he staid in Jerusalem, and that he did so, and then came back to his post at the cross.

At noon a change comes on the scene. The three who hang on the cross still live, and the crowd still surge at the foot and send up their jeers and taunts at him who hangs in the midst. But all at once all grows dark. The sun hides its face, not in clouds which soon drift by and leave it clear and bright; but for three long hours there is no light.

The hush of death rests on the PLACE OF A SKULL. But at the ninth hour (that is at three o'clock) Jesus cried out with a loud voice, "My God! My God! why hast thou left me!" It was not mere pain which wrung that cry from his heart, but the same woe which he had borne in Gethsemane. It was the sins of the world.

Then he cried, "I thirst," and some one who stood by wet a sponge in sour wine, and put it on a long reed, so that it could reach his lips, and he drank. Then Jesus who knew that all which the word of God had said that the Christ must do and bear, had now been done, said, "It is done," and then with a loud cry to God, he bent his head on his breast and gave up the ghost.

At that last cry the earth shook; the rocks were rent, and the veil of

God's, house was torn in twain, in the midst and the graves gave up their dead.

Then came a new proof that Jesus Christ on his cross will draw all men to him. The chief of the squad of troops who stood by to watch the scene, and those who were with him, when they saw what was done cried, " In truth this was the Son of God!" And the crowd who had come out to see the sight, and had been so light of heart and full of taunts and jeers, now smite on their breasts in fear and shame as they go to their homes. And far off, yet where they could see all that was done, stood a large group of the friends of Jesus, and not a few of the wives and maids from his old home in Galilee, who had been with him in his last tour or had come up to Jerusalem to meet him here.

Some of the Jews who did not know that Jesus was dead, and who did not wish that the cross should still stand on God's day which now drew near, went to Pilate to beg that he would have his men of war break the legs of those who hung there, and thus put a quick end to their life. So they broke the legs of the two thieves, but when they came to Jesus they found him dead, so they did not break a bone of him, as it had been said of him, like the lamb slain for the feast, " They shall not break a bone of him." But one of the guards took his spear and thrust it in his side, from which blood come forth.

Now we come to the third proof that Jesus Christ on the cross would draw all men to him.

There was a rich man, Joseph of Arimathea, a judge of high rank, and " a good man and just," whose faith in Jesus (which had been hid " for fear of the Jews,") is made to blaze out in the sight of all men by his death on the cross. While he lives, and works great signs, and speaks grand words Joseph dare not own him, though he loves him in his heart. But as soon as his foes seem to have had their own way and to have made an end of him and his work, Joseph's faith grows frank and strong and bold. He goes right to Pilate who knows him well, and begs for leave to take the corpse of Jesus. Pilate does not know what to make of it when he hears that Jesus is so soon dead. Death on the cross is a slow mode of death, and Jesus had hung there but six hours at the most. Pilate sends for the chief of his troops who were there to watch the scene, and learns from him that it is so in truth. Then he gives Joseph leave to do what he asks.

But when Joseph goes to claim his prize, he is met by one who longs to share in the last sad rites. Nicodemus (he who went to Jesus by night for fear of the Jews, two or three years back), rich, and of the same high rank with Joseph, now comes to do his best to show his faith in him. He brings with him five score pounds of rare drugs to wrap round the corpse of Jesus, which is the way in which the rich Jews show their love for their dead friends.

Joseph's own grounds are near at hand, and in them is a new tomb which he has had hewn out of the rock, but where no one has as yet been laid.

So when Nicodemus and Joseph have wrapt the limbs of Jesus in soft fine bands and the rare drugs, they lay him in the tomb, and roll a great stone to the door, and make haste back to the town, that they may reach it ere the first hour of God's day shall strike, which will be at six o'clock of the night of that same day on which Jesus died.

Mary Magdalene, and the rest who came from Galilee with Jesus, staid by till they had seen their Lord laid to rest in the rich man's tomb, and then they, too, had to go home to keep the Day.

But though Jesus is dead, though he has died in the sight of such a crowd of men, yet his foes still fear him. So as quick as the sun sets on God's day, they rush off to Pilate with a new cry. "Sir," they say, "we call to mind that that man said, in his life time, 'In three days I will rise from the dead.' Now let the tomb be made sure till the third day is past, lest his friends come by night and steal him, and then say that he rose from the dead."

Pilate said to them, "You have a watch; go your way; make it as sure as ye can."

So they went and made the tomb

sure, and put their seal on the stone, so they could know if one should try to move it. And then, to make all more sure, they add to the watch who are to march up and down with their arms, in front of the dead man's tomb. How sure they are of him now!

On the first day of the week (which from that day to this is known as the Lord's Day), when it was yet dark, but as dawn drew near, Mary Magdalene and her friend Mary set out for the tomb of their Lord, with the sweet spice which they had brought too late on the night of Christ's death to use.

The five score pounds' weight which they knew Nicodemus brought, is not their gift, and they long to pour out their all to grace his tomb.

We lay wreaths on the graves of those most dear to us, but in the land of the Jews, sweet drugs took the place of sweet blooms.

While these fond friends are on their way to the tomb, a strange scene takes place at that spot of Jesus' rest.

The earth shakes; one of God's hosts comes down from on high, rolls back the great stone from the door of the tomb, and sits on it. His face is like the light, and his robes are white as snow. The guards, who see this dread sight, shake with fear, and fall to the ground like dead men.

Saints who have slept in the grave for years and years, come forth and walk through the streets of Jerusalem, and are seen of not a few who dwell there.

Now, as Mary and her friends get near the place where Jesus had been laid, all at once they call to mind how great the stone was which they had seen put at the door of the tomb, and say, " Who will roll the stone from the door of the tomb for us?"

But as they come up to the great rock in which the tomb is cleft, they see that the stone is gone! Mary Magdalene, in her grief and fear lest the dear corpse of her Lord has come to harm, does not wait to look through the door of the tomb, but flies back to Jerusalem and finds Peter and John and tells her sad tale, " They have borne off the Lord from his tomb, and we know not where they have laid him!"

But the two friends whom Mary

Magdalene left at the tomb, go in to see if they can not find some trace of their Lord. There sits a young man clad in a long white robe, who calms their fears at once.

"Fear not," he says; "I know that ye seek Jesus of Nazareth, who died on the cross. He is not here. He rose from the dead, as he said he would do. Come, see the place where the Lord lay. But go your way with speed and tell his friends and Peter, that he rose from the dead, and will meet you in Galilee. There shall ye see him, as he said to you. Lo! I have told you."

And they went out with haste from the tomb, and with fear, and dare speak to no one by the way; but ran with the good news to Jesus' friends.

In the mean time Peter and John have set out in great haste to see with their own eyes what Mary Magdalene had told them of.

They both ran, but John got to the tomb first, and bent down to look in. He saw no one, but there lay the fine white bands in which fond hands had wrapt Jesus the night of his death. But Peter, when he came up, did not stop at the door. He went right in the tomb, and saw the clothes. These clothes did not look as if they had been torn off in haste, but they lay in neat folds, each in its place. Then John went in, and he saw these things, and knew that Jesus had left the grave of his own free will.

Then Peter and John went back to their own home. But Mary Magdalene did not go. She staid to weep. The glad thought that Jesus could and must rise from the dead to prove the truth of all that he had said and done, has not as yet made its way to her heart. She clings to the sad thought that the foes of Jesus must have come to steal his corpse for some bad end of their own, and that she can not strew the sweet gifts she had brought on his grave.

As she weeps, she stoops down to look in, and sees two Forms of light, who sit on each side of the place where Jesus had lain. They say to her, "Why dost thou weep?"

"They have borne off my Lord, and I know not where they have laid him."

When she had said this, she turns

her head and sees Jesus, who stands near her. But her heart is so full of fear and grief, and her eyes of tears, that she does not know him. She thinks he must be the man who has charge of Joseph's grounds, and says to him, " Sir, if thou hast borne him hence, tell me where thou hast laid him, and I will take care of him."

" Mary!"

What a thrill the well known voice of Jesus must have sent through that sad heart of hers!

She falls down and tries to clasp his feet, but all she can say is, " My Lord!" But Jesus bids her touch him not, for he has not yet gone up on high. But he bids her, too, go and tell his friends that he will soon go back to his God and their God.

On her way, Salome and Mary 2d join her, and Jesus meets them and bids them " Fear not, but go and tell my friends to go to Galilee, and there shall they see me."

But when they tell his friends of what they have seen and heard, they have no faith in their words.

That same day, two friends of Jesus' were on their way to Emmaus, which was eight miles from Jerusalem. As they walk, they talk of the sad scenes in Pilate's hall, on the road to Calvary, and of the death on the cross. In the midst of this talk one joins them whom they know not (it is said that their eyes were held so they did not know him), and asks them why they are so sad.

Cleopas (that is the name of one of

them) said that " He who asks this can not have been in Jerusalem, since he does not know the things which have come to pass there in these days?"

"What things?" asks their new friend.

"Why how Jesus of Nazareth, who spoke such words and wrought such great deeds in the sight of all men, has been put to death on the cross by our chief priests and those who rule us. Our hope was that it had been he who should save Israel, and this is the third day since these things were done. Some of our friends who went to his tomb at dawn, found that he was not there, and say that they saw Forms of Light, and were told by them that Jesus still lives."

He who had met them heard them

through, and then said, "O fools and slow of heart, to trust all the words which ye have heard as to Christ and his work! Ought not Christ to have borne all these things to prove his claims?"

And then he went back to what Moses and men of old wrote of Christ, that he might show them how all things had been done by Jesus of Nazareth which it had been said the Christ should do. But still their eyes were held, and they knew him not.

When they came to Emmaus, he made as if he would have gone on, but they beg him to stay with them. They know not who he is, but they feel that it is good to be with him. When they urge that the day is far spent and the night draws on, he turns in with them to the house where they are to stay. But their guest is soon their host; for it came to pass as he sat at meat with them he took bread and did bless it, and brake and gave to them. Now their eyes are held no more, and they know their Lord! But as they gaze at him in awe and love, he fades from their sight, and they see him no more. Then how they call up all his words and looks by the way, and cry, " Did not our hearts burn as he spoke with us by the way?" And they rose up that same hour, though night drew on, and went back to Jerusalem to tell their friends what things were done in the way, and how Christ was made known to them as he broke the bread.

That same night the friends of

Christ met by stealth, and with shut doors, for fear of the Jews. All at once Jesus stood in their midst with the words, " Peace be with you!" They are in great fear at this sight, and think it is his ghost, for he has made his way to them in spite of shut doors and bolts and bars.

But Jesus said, " Why do you fear? and why do such thoughts rise in your hearts? See my hands and my feet that it is I; touch me and see; for a ghost hath not flesh and bones as ye see me have."

When he shows them his hands and feet with the rents which the nails of the cross had made in them, and the wound of the spear in his side, then were they glad, as they saw the Lord. To make them still more sure that it is not his ghost, he asks for food, and eats in their sight.

Then once more Jesus said, " Peace be to you ! as God hath sent me forth, so send I you," and as he breathes on them he gives them the HOLY GHOST.

Now, there was one of the twelve who was not at the place where they met that night, and when those who had been there told him what he had lost, he doubts their word. He said, " I shall have no faith that it is he if I can not see in his hands the print of the nails, and touch the prints of the nails, and thrust my hand in his side !"

But the next week, when they met on what has been known from the day when Christ rose from the dead till now, as the Lord's day, Thomas was there.

When all were in and the doors shut, Jesus stands forth in their midst, and says, " Peace be to you!" Then he turns to Thomas, whose head doubts, though his heart loves, and says, " See and touch the prints of the nails! Thrust thy hand in my side, and doubt no more, but have faith in me!"

Thomas' doubts all fly at these words. He does not care to see or touch the wounds of his Lord's flesh, for he sees through that torn flesh the GOD WITH US of whom Isaiah sung, and cries "My Lord, and my God!"

Christ next meets his friends as he had told them he would, in a mount, in Galilee. His school seem not to have yet seen what Jesus meant to have them do. They do not break up, and yet some of them seem to have gone back to their old trades. Peter, at least, as he stands once more on the shore of the Lake of Galilee feels his old thirst come back, and cries out " I shall go and fish!" Four or five of Christ's school who chance to be with him at the time, say, " We will go with thee." So they sail out on the lake and toil all night, but catch no fish.

At dawn Jesus stood on the shore, but they knew him not. Nor do they know him when he asks if they have caught no fish. When they tell him that they have not, he bids them cast their net on the right side of the ship and they shall find fish. Still they know not that it is Jesus, but as they throw the net where he bade them, it fills with fish at once, so that they can not draw the net back on board the boat! Then John said to Peter "It is the Lord!"

Peter cares no more for the fish when he hears that glad word. He caught up his coat which he had laid off in his toil, and sprang into the sea, and made for the shore as fast as he could. The rest of the crew come on in the boat, and drag the net with them. When they reach the shore they find a fire of coals, and fish laid on it, and bread. Jesus bids them bring some of the fish from the net and they find it full. There are not far from eight score great fish, and yet the net does not break. Then Jesus said to them, "Come and dine," and they drew near, but dare not speak to him.

Jesus now acts as their host. He took bread and gave to them, and fish as well.

When the meal is done, Jesus turns to Peter and speaks words which must have been like balm to his sore heart. Peter's grief is still fresh for the wrong he had done his Lord, when he said three times that he knew him not, in the dark hour when he was left to trust to his own weak heart. But he now hears him to whom he had been so false, say, in mild, sweet tones, " Simon, son of Jonas, dost thou love me more than these?"

Peter is not so rash as he was, and does not boast of his love, but he is sure of it, " Yes, Lord, thou dost know that I love thee." Jesus then shows him how he can make proof of his love; "Feed my lambs." Help the young and the weak to find their strength and life in your Lord. But Jesus asks once more, in the same words. "Simon, son of Jonas, dost thou love me?"

"Yes, Lord; thou dost know that I love thee."

"Feed my sheep."

The third time Jesus asks, "Simon, son of Jona, dost thou love me!"

Three times Peter has said, of Jesus, "I know not the man," and three times he must own his love to Jesus. Peter grieves that his Lord should ask him this the third time, but says with all his heart, "Lord, thou dost know all things; thou dost know that I love thee."

"Feed my sheep."

Then Jesus tells Peter by what mode of death he will die, in these words; " When thou wert young thou didst gird thee, and walk where thou didst please ; but when thou shalt be old strange hands will gird thee and bear thee where thou wouldst not."

And so it came to pass, for Peter was to serve Christ all his life, and prove his love to him when an old man, by death, for his name's sake. Bad men would " gird" him, as they had bound his Lord, to the cross.

There are two things which are told of Peter, which seem as if they must be true, though they are not found in God's word. It is said that through all Peter's long life he could not hear a cock crow but it would thrill his heart with the thought of his base lies on the day when Christ was tried for his life; and he would at once fall on his knees and pray that that foul sin might not be laid to his charge. Then, too, it is said, that when the hour came for him to be made fast to the cross on which he was to die, the same thought of how false he had been to his Lord clung to him, and made him beg those who were to nail him to the wood to place him with his head down, for he said he was not fit to die by the same death with his Lord.

When Peter has heard what his own fate is to be he wants to know what will come to John. He knows how fond Jesus has been of John who sat with his head on his Lord's breast at their last feast, and so he asks, "Lord, and what shall this man do?"

Jesus does not choose to tell. " If I will that he stay till I come, what is that to thee?"

John who tells us this, says, that some who heard it thought Jesus meant by this that John should not die, but states that that was not what Christ said at all but, " If I will that he stay till I come, what is that to thee?"

Once more Jesus met his school at Jerusalem, and told them what their work in the world was to be. Not to fish or to take tolls, but to spread the good news in Jerusalem first, and then through all the world. He bids them stay in Jerusalem till the HOLY GHOST shall come down on them to fit them for this great work, and then go forth and preach in his name.

Jesus staid on earth two score days from the day when he rose from the dead. He gave proof on proof that he was the same Jesus who had died on the cross. He made them see at last what all his life had not taught them, that he was in truth, the King of kings, though not like this world's kings, and that they were to spread his realm till it should take in all the world. He told them too, that in this great work, though he would be hid from their sight, yet he would be with them. "Lo I am with you at all times, to the end of the world." And when he had thus taught them, and made them strong in the faith, he left them to do his work.

He leads them out as far as Bethany, and there lifts up his hands to bless them. While he thus stands with eyes that beam with love, and hands that bless, he floats through the air up and up and up, till a cloud veils him from their sight! It is not strange that this weak band should stand and gaze and gaze in hope that they may yet catch a wave of those hands which bless to the last, or a glimpse of the robe which shrouds his form. But they look in vain. A voice at their side brings their eyes back to earth. There stood with them two men in white robes who say, "Ye men of Galilee, why stand ye and thus gaze? This same Jesus who has thus gone from your sight, shall come once more as ye have seen him go."

So they went back to Jerusalem with great joy, and spent their time in

God's house to praise and bless God. Then when the HOLY GHOST came on them they went forth to preach in all lands and the Lord wrought with them, and still works, and will work with those who seek to do His WORK till the end of the world.

*Interesting and Beautiful Books for Children,*

# PUBLISHED BY GEO. A. LEAVITT,

No. 8 HOWARD STREET, NEW YORK,

*And which may be had at any Bookstore, or will be sent by mail free on receipt of the published price.*

An Entire New Series of

## NURSERY BIBLE BOOKS

### IN WORDS OF ONE SYLLABLE.

Printed in large type, and each book beautifully illustrated with 10 full page engravings, printed in Oil Colors.

*THE PILGRIM'S PROGRESS* from this World to that which is to Come. By JOHN BUNYAN. In Words of One Syllable for Children. By Mrs. EDWARD ASHLEY WALKER, author of "Watson's Woods," "Our Little Girls," etc., etc., 336 pages, 16mo quarto, and Illustrated by 10 beautiful Engravings printed in Oil Colors. . . Extra Cloth, $1.50

*FROM THE CRIB TO THE CROSS.* A Life of Christ in Words of one Syllable, for children. By Mrs. EDWARD ASHLEY WALKER. 320 pages 16mo quarto, with 10 beautiful Illustrations printed in Oil Colors. Extra Cloth, $1.50

*FROM THE CREATION TO MOSES.* Bible Stories from the Old Testament, and in Bible language as far as possible. Contains the Creation—Garden of Eden—Noah's Ark—Story of Joseph and his Brethren—Abraham, the friend of God, etc. By Mrs. FRED G. BURNHAM, author of "Earnest," etc., etc.

*FROM MOSES TO DANIEL.* A Second Series of Bible Stories from the Old Testament. Containing the Story of Ruth—Story of David—Story of Samson—Story of Saul—Story of Joshua—Story of Daniel, etc. By Mrs. FRED. G. BURNHAM. Uniform with "From the Creation," etc.

## IN PRESS.

*FROM MATTHEW TO JOHN.* Bible Stories from the New Testament.

*THE PARABLES OF OUR LORD.*

*THE MIRACLES OF OUR LORD.*

*LIFE OF ST. PAUL.*

*JOSEPH AND HIS BRETHREN*, etc., etc.

Each of the above will contain about 320 pages, large type and beautifully Illustrated, square 16mo, extra cloth.

---

*TIP-TOP STORY BOOKS.* For Boys and Girls. By Mrs. L. C. TUTHILL.

Tip-Top Story Books for Boys.
    *Tip-Top.*      *Braggadocio.*      *Get Money.*

3 vols. 16mo, in box, extra cloth. Illustrated, . . per vol. $1 25

Tip-Top Story Books for Girls.
    *Queer Bonnets.*      *Edith; or, the Backwoods Girl.*
               *Beautiful Bertha.*

3 vols. 16mo, in box, extra cloth. Illustrated, . . per vol. 1 25

---

*THE BO-PEEP STORY BOOKS.* 6 vols., square 16mo, extra cloth, in a neat box, . . . . . per set 2 50

Containing fifty of the most popular Fairy Tales.

*The Children in the Wood.*     *The White Cat.*
*Little Red Riding Hood.*     *John Gilpin.*
*Jack and the Bean Stalk.*     *Cinderella.*
*Jack the Giant Killer.*     *Reynard the Fox.*
             *Etc., Etc.*

*THE BO-PEEP LIBRARY.* 3 vols., square 16mo, in a neat box, new style and illuminated cover, extra cloth, per set, . 2 00

Same as the Bo-Peep Story Books, bound in 3 volumes instead of 6.

*Price List, Geo. A. Leavitt, Publisher.* 3

*LITTLE ONES' LIBRARY.* 6 vols., 48mo, with brightly-colored pictures. Bound in extra cloth, gilt back, and in handsome box, new style, Illuminated cover, . . . . . per set $1 50

*The Summer House.*   *Kriss Kringle.*
*The Robins.*   *The Bird's Nest.*
*The Skating Party.*   *The Omnibus.*

*THE BIRD'S NEST SERIES.* 3 vols., 48mo, with brightly colored pictures, extra cloth, in a neat box, . . per set 1 00
Same as Little Ones' Library, bound in 3 volumes.

*LITTLE PET LIBRARY.* 6 vols., 64mo, full of pictures. Bound in extra cloth, gilt back, and in a handsome box, new style, Illuminated cover, . . . . . . . per set 1 25

*The Girl and her Pets.*   *The Boy and his Pony.*
*The Sailor Boy.*   *Book of Stories.*
*Book of Sports.*   *Book of Trades.*

*CHILD'S PET BOOKS.* 3 vols., 64mo, full of pictures. Bound in extra cloth, gilt back, and in a neat box, . . per set 75c.
Same as Little Pet Library, bound in 3 volumes.

*·LITTLE CHILD'S KEEPSAKE.* 1 vol. 48mo, full of brighty colored pictures, extra cloth, full gilt and gilt edges, . . . 1 00

*LITTLE PET KEEPSAKE.* 1 vol. 48mo, full of pictures, extra cloth, full gilt and gilt edges, . . . . . . 75c.

*MY FAVORITE STORY BOOKS.* 12 vols., square 16mo, brightly-colored pictures, extra cloth, in neat box, . . per set 5.00

*Harry's Stories.*   *Book of True Stories.*
*The Troubadour.*   *Juvenile Sports.*
*Cousin Agnes' Stories.*   *Mocking Bird.*
*Carries Pigeon.*   *Aunt Ellen's Visit.*
*Lady Beautiful.*   *The Emigrant.*
*Country Scenes.*   *The Good Shepherd.*

*THE "CHILD'S OWN BOOK SERIES."* 6 volumes, 16mo,
in neat case. Each volume illustrated and handsomely bound in cloth
extra, . . . . . . . . . . . $1 25
The cheapest set of Juveniles published, 2,500 pages of reading for $6.25.
Retail.

 *Child's Own Book of Merry Tales.*
  *Boys' Own Book of Sports, Birds and Animals.*
   *Child's Own Book of Fairy Tales and Rhymes.*
   *Child's Own Book of Pictures and Stories.*
  *Boys' and Girls' Own Story Book.*
 *Child's Own Fable Book.*

The above are six of the best books of the kind for Children published.
Comprise all the popular Juvenile Fairy Tales, besides a profuse amount of
interesting and entertaining matter.

*BOYS' AND GIRLS' BOOKS OF PICTURES & STORIES.*
3 vols., large 16mo, each volume illustrated and handsomely bound in
extra cloth; put up in a handsome case, new style, and illuminated cover
for presents, . . . . . . . . per vol. 1.25

The above two Series of Children's Books are the best of the kind published. Comprising all the Popular Juvenile Fairy Tales, besides a profuse
amount of interesting and entertaining matter.

*THE BOYS' OWN BOOKS.* 3 vols. in neat case, and
handsomely bound in cloth extra. . . . . Per set. 2 25

*Boys' Book of Animals.*    *Boys' Book of Birds.*
  *Boys' Book of Sports.*
  Three cheap, useful and interesting volumes.

*MAMA'S PICTURE BOOK.* 1 vol., quarto, brightly-
colored engravings, handsomely bound in cloth exra. . . . 1 50

 *Hunters and Hunting.*    *Scenes in Europe.*
 *Fables for Children.*    *Scenes in Africa.*
 *Snow and Ice.*    *Animals.*

# HEADLEY'S ILLUSTRATED BIOGRAPHIES.

**PROMINENT HEROES OF THE LATE WAR.**

A Series of Biographies of Modern American Heroes, written expressly for Boys and Young Men. By Rev. P. C. HEADLEY.

Each volume is thoroughly *reliable* and *authentic*, Mr. H. having, direct from the heroes in question and their relatives, material and facts not to be obtained by any one party.

## GRANT—SHERMAN—SHERIDAN.

*The Hero Boy.* 1 vol., 16mo, cloth, 367 pp. illustrated, 1 25
Being the Life and Deeds of GEN. ULYSSES S. GRANT, the Patriot and Hero. Tracing his career from Boyhood to Manhood, from the School-house to President of the United States. 1 25

*Sherman and his Battles.* 1 vol. 16mo, cloth, 350 pp. Illustrated. . . . . . . . . . 1 25
A Boy's Life of Major-General W. T. SHERMAN.

*Sheridan, the Soldier and Hero.* 1 vol. 16mo, cloth, 368 pp. Illustrated. . . . . . . . . 1 25
A Boy's Life of Major-General P. H. SHERIDAN.

## FARRAGUT—ERICSSON—MITCHELL.

*Farragut, First in Rank and First in Battle,* 1 vol. 16mo, cloth, 350 pp. Illustrated. . . . . . . . 1 25
A Boy's Life of Vice-Admiral FARRAGUT.

*The Miner Boy and his Monitor.* 1 vol. 16mo, cloth, 300 pp. Illustrated. . . . . . . . . . 1 25
A Boy's Life of Captain ERICSSON, the Inventor of the Famous Monitor.

*The Patriot Boy.* 1 vol. 16mo, cloth, 300 pp. Illustratrated. . . . . . . . . . . 1 25
Being the life of Major-General O. M. MITCHELL, the Astronomer and Hero.

NO HOUSEHOLD SHOULD BE WITHOUT THEM.

*Grant — Sherman — Sheridan.*

The 3 volumes in a handsome box, bound in extra cloth, gilt back. Illustrated with fine engravings, . . . . . Per set 3 75

*Farragut — Ericsson — Mitchell.*

The 3 volumes in a handsome box, bound in extra cloth, gilt back, handsomely illustrated, with fine engravings. . . . Per set 3 75

The above books should be read by every boy and young man in the country.

---

## THE GIRLS AND MOTHERS OF THE BIBLE.

2 vols. royal 16mo, cloth extra, and illustrated with fine steel engravings, . . . . . . . . . Per vol. 1 25

Interesting, Useful and Instructive.

*Girls of the Bible.* By P. C. HEADLEY.

*Mothers of the Bible.* By Mrs. ASHTON.

## THE KATIE STORY BOOKS. 4 vols. small 16mo.

Each volume profusely illustrated, handsomely bound in extra cloth, gilt back, in a handsome case, new style, with illuminated cover. Per set . . . . . . . . . . 2 00

*The Rich and the Poor, etc.*   *Skipping Hard Words, etc.*
*The Cruel Landlord, etc.*   *The Little Story Teller, etc.*

A series of pretty books, good reading, and full of pictures.

## THE WILLIE STORY BOOKS. 4 vols. small 16mo,

handsomely bound in extra cloth, gilt back, and put up in a handsome case, new style, with illuminated cover. . . . Per set 2 00

*Pretty Stories for Willie.*
*The Good Son, etc.*
*Little Painter and Spruce Johnnie.*
*Pretty Stories for Good Boys.*

A series of short and pretty stories, each volume full of illustrations.

## THE GOOD STORY BOOK. 4 vols. small 16mo,

handsomely bound in extra cloth, gilt back, and put up in a handsome case, new style, with illuminated cover. . . . Per set 2 00

*Juvenile Sports.*   *Good Little Stories.*
*Little Rhyme Book.*   *Reward of Kindness.*

Short and good Stories for Girls and Boys.

## LITTLE GIRLS' AND BOYS' LIBRARY.
6 vols., small 16mo, handsomely bound in extra cloth, gilt back, and put up in a handsome case, new style, with illuminated cover. Per set 3 00

*Minnie, the Broom Girl.*   *Two Bad Boys, etc.*
*Walter O'Neil.*   *My Menagerie—Birds.*
*Stuart and Helen Bruce.*   *My Menagerie—Animals.*
*Stories in Rhyme.*

Interesting, useful, and good stories, profusely illustrated.

## UGLY DUCKLING STORY BOOKS.
3 vols., square 12mo, handsomely bound in extra cloth, all bright colors, and in a neat case.   .   .   .   .   .   .   . Per set 2 50

*The Ugly Duckling.*
*Puss in Boots.*
*Little Old Woman who Lived in a Shoe.*
*Little Bo-Peep.*
*Dan Drake's Rhymes.*
*Children's Fables.*

A series of very beautiful books, in new square 12mo size, printed on the finest paper, and filled with very prettily-colored engravings; very cheap popular books.

A remarkably cheap and beautiful set of books.

## THE LILLIE STORY BOOKS.  16mo, full of illustrations.

LILLIE'S DAY. A new set of Juveniles, 6 vols., 16mo, printed on elegant paper and handsomely bound in cloth extra, and in neat case.   .   .   .   .   .   .   . Per set 2 50

*Lillie's Day.*
*Lillie's People Abroad.*
*Lillie's Visit to the Menagerie.*
*Lillie's Bird Garden.*
*Lillie's Stories About Indians.*
*Lillie's Pigeon House.*

LILLIE'S EVENING. A new set of Juveniles, 6 vols., 16mo, full of illustrations, printed on elegant paper and handsomely bound in cloth extra, and a neat case. . . . . Per set 2 50

*Lillie's Evening.*            *Lillie's Grandfather.*
*Lillie's Aunt Lucy.*        *Lillie's Little Housewife.*
*Lillie's Canary.*            *Lillie's Naughty Brother.*

THE FORGET-ME-NOT LIBRARY. 3 vols., 16mo, in handsome case, new style, illuminated cover, and illustrated with fine steel engravings, and handsomely bound in extra cloth, new and beautiful style for presents. . . . . . . . Per set 3 00

*Juvenile Forget-Me-Not.*      *The Rosebud.*
*The Violet.*

A handsome series of books adapted for presents.

THE KEEPSAKE LIBRARY. 3 vols., 16mo, in neat case, new style, illuminated cover, and handsomely bound in extra cloth. New and beautiful style for presents. . . . . Per set 3 00

*The Youth's Keepsake.*      *The Humming Bird.*
*The Pet Animal.*

Three handsome volumes, bound in a new and beautiful style.

THE KRISS KRINGLE STORY BOOKS. 3 vols., square 16mo, handsomely bound in extra cloth, gilt back, new and beautiful style for presents, in handsome case, new style, illuminated cover. Per set 3 00

The same. Elegantly bound in fine cloth, gilt side, gilt edges, 3 vols. in handsome case. . . . . . . . Per set 4 00

*Kriss Kringle's Story Book.*     *St. Nicholas' Story Book.*
*Santa Claus' Story Book.*

A series of charming books for youths, girls, or boys, illustrated with fine steel engravings and bound in a new and very handsome style.

*SANTA CLAUS' FAIRY STORY BOOKS.* 6 vols., square 16mo, handsomely bound in cloth extra, in neat case. . Per set 5 00

 *Arabian Nights.*     *Gulliver's Travels.*
 *Fairy Godmother.*    *Fable Land.*
 *Æsop's Fables.*      *Fairy Tales.*

  Beautiful editions of standard juvenile books

*THE GULLIVER LIBRARY.* 3 vols., square 16mo, bound in extra cloth, and put up in a handsome box, new style, and illuminated cover. . . . . . . . . Per set 2 50

 *Gulliver's Travels.*    *Arabian Nights.*
    *Æsop's Fables.*

  Three of the most popular of juvenile books.

*AUNT FANNY.—THE SOCK STORIES.* 6 vols., square 16mo, illustrated, and bound in cloth extra, in neat case. Per set 5 00

 *Blue, White and Red Socks. Part I.*
 *Funny Little Socks.*
  *Blue, White and Red Socks. Part II.*
  *Funny Big Socks.*
  *German Socks.*
  *Neighbor Nellie's Socks.*

  The most popular of writers for the amusement of children.

*AUNT MARY'S STORY BOOKS.* 6 vols., 16mo, handsomely illustrated and bound in cloth extra. . . Per set 4 50

 *Aunt Mary's Stories.*    *Gift Story Book.*
 *Frank and Fanny.*     *Parley's New York.*
 *Peep at Birds.*       *Peep at Beasts.*

*MOTHER GOOSE'S MELODIES.* Square 16mo, stiff paper cover. . . . . . . . . Per copy 20
THE SAME. Bound in cloth extra. . . . . Per copy · 50

  Best and pure edition of Mother Goose.

#### A NEW AND UNIQUE SET OF BOOKS.

*THE MAGIC PICTURE BOOKS.* In six volumes, small quarto, colored plates. This is an entirely new and unique set of books, each volume contains 12 handsomely colored illustrations, with 144 changes, making 144 highly amusing and comic pictures, handsomely bound, illuminated boards. . . . . . Per vol. $0 50

*CHILDREN'S SCRAP BOOK.* Complete in 1 vol., quarto, containing nearly 1,000 plates, brightly colored, cloth extra. . 3 00

*ALL THE CHILDREN'S NURSERY RHYME BOOK.* Cloth, gilt . . . . . . . . . . . 75

*ÆSOP'S FABLES.* Full of illustrations, 16mo, cloth extra. . . . . . . . . . . 75

*ARABIAN NIGHTS.* Illustrated, 16mo, cloth extra, 75

*GULLIVER'S TRAVELS.* Illustrated, 16mo, cloth extra . . . . . . . . . . . 75

*PICTURE GIFT BOOK.* Large 4to, 200 beautifully colored engravings, cloth extra . . . . . . . . 2 00

*PICTURE BOOK FOR GOOD BOYS AND GIRLS.* Large 4to, 200 colored engravings, fancy boards . . . . 2 00

## Cheap and Attractive Books.

*PRETTY PICTURES AND PLEASANT RHYMES.* Large 4to, 150 colored engravings, fancy boards - - - - 1 00

*CHILD'S SCRAP BOOK.* Large 4to, 150 colored engravings, fancy boards, . . . . . . . . 1 00

*PICTORIAL GIFT FOR LITTLE ONES.* Large 4to, 150 colored engravings, fancy boards, . . . . . . 1 00

*BOY'S HANDY BOOK OF GAMES, SPORTS, PASTIMES,* and Amusements; being a complete Encyclopædia of Boyish Recreative Pursuits of every description, and forming a guide to the Employment of every Leisure Hour. Full of illustrations and handsomely bound in extra cloth, full gilt side and edges. 348 pages, post 8vo . . $3 00

The best Book of Games. One of the most popular and salable Juvenile Books published.

*NURSERY RHYMES, OLD AND NEW.* A collection of the most Favorite Nursery Rhymes, Jingles and Stories; also, many New Ones now for the first time printed. Imperial 32mo, numerous clever and characteristic illustrations, extra cloth, gilt sides, back and edges . 2 50

*EVENINGS AT HOME;* or, *THE JUVENILE BUDGET OPENED.* Consisting of a variety of Miscellaneous Pieces for the Instruction and Amusement of Young Persons. By Dr. Aiken and Mrs. Barbauld. Extra cloth, gilt side, back and edges, full of illustrations, . . . . . . . . . . 2 00

The best and cheapest edition of this style published. Full of illustrations and handsomely bound in extra cloth, full gilt side and edges. Royal 16mo.

*THE LIFE AND SURPRISING ADVENTURES OF ROBINSON CRUSOE,* of York, Mariner. By Daniel De Foe. With a Biographical Sketch of the Author. Embellished with a great number of engravings on wood. Extra cloth, gilt side, back and edges. . 2 00

*THE HISTORY OF SANFORD AND MERTON.* By Thomas Day. Illustrated with 100 engravings by the Brothers Dalziel. Extra cloth, gilt side, back and edges, . . . . . 2 00

*BUNYAN'S PILGRIM'S PROGRESS* from this World to that which is to come. A new edition, with a Memoir. Illustrated with 100 engravings by the Brothers Dalziel. Extra cloth, gilt side, back and edges. . . . . . . . . . . 2 00

## The Standard Favorite Series.

In small 8vo, printed on toned paper, richly bound in cloth and gold and gilt edges, with new and original Frontispiece, printed in colors.

*THE VICAR OF WAKEFIELD.* Poems and Essays. By Oliver Goldsmith.

*BUNYAN'S PILGRIM'S PROGRESS.*

*THE LIFE AND ADVENTURES OF ROBINSON CRUSOE.*

*ÆSOP'S FABLES.* With instructive Applications. By Dr. Croxall.

*THE HISTORY OF SANFORD AND MERTON.*

*EVENINGS AT HOME; or, THE JUVENILE BUDGET OPENED.* 6 vols., in neat case, bound in cloth and gold, gilt edges.

Per vol. $1 50

The above are very elegant and remarkably cheap editions of these old favorite Works.

## The Little Crusoe Library.

Beautiful editions of these popular books. Demy 18mo, illustrated, cloth extra, full gilt side and gilt edges.

*THE VICAR OF WAKEFIELD.* Poems and Essays. By Oliver Goldsmith.

*ÆSOP'S FABLES.* With Instructive Applications. By Dr. Croxall.

*BUNYAN'S PILGRIM'S PROGRESS.*

*THE LIFE AND ADVENTURES OF ROBINSON CRUSOE.*

*THE HISTORY OF SANFORD AND MERTON.*

*EVENINGS AT HOME; or, THE JUVENILE BUDGET OPENED.*

*UNEXPECTED PLEASURES.*

*TREASURY ANECDOTES.*

Eight volumes, beautifully bound in cloth and gold, gilt edges, in neat case. . . . . . . . . . Per vol. $0 90

The above series of elegant and useful books are specially prepared for the entertainment and instruction of young persons.

## INDESTRUCTIBLE AND BEAUTIFUL

# TOY BOOKS FOR CHILDREN,

Now manufactured exclusively for Geo. A. Leavitt, by Geo. R. Mooney, 97 Cliff street, New York, the original manufacturer of the well-known "Indestructible Books" for children, printed on linen cloth in oil colors, and in addition to the "Indestructible Books," the subscriber offers a large variety of Toy Books, on paper, also printed in colors.

*INDESTRUCTIBLE TOY BOOKS.* Printed on linen cloth in oil colors, and assorted in dozens, as follows:

    *The House that Jack Built.*
    *Old Mother Hubbard and her Dog.*
    *Little Bo-Peep and Henny Penny*
    *The Three Bears.*
    *Cock Robin and Jenny Wren.*
    *Mother Goose and Simple Simon.*

                             Price, per dozen 3 75

*INDESTRUCTIBLE NURSERY RHYMES.* Printed on linen cloth in oil colors, and assorted in dozens, as follows:

    *Aunt Mary's Nursery Rhymes.*
    *Aunt Kitty's Nursery Rhymes.*
    *Aunt Jenny's Nursery Rhymes.*

                             Price, per dozen 3 75

*INDESTRUCTIBLE PRIMERS.* Printed on linen cloth in oil colors:

    *The Boy's and Girl's Primer.*
       *The Bible Alphabet.*
          *The Farmer Boy's Alphabet.*

Each book contains Alphabets and Spelling and Reading Lessons.
                                      Price, per dozen $3 75

*RHYMES WITHOUT REASON.* Printed in oil colors, with illustrations, by C. H. Bennett. . . Price, per dozen 2 00

*UNTEARABLE OCTAVO BOOKS.* Printed on the finest paper. Four kinds in oil colors:

    *Little Bo-Peep.*
       *Three Bears.*
          *Little Man and Maid.*
             *Old Woman and her Pig.*
                                      Price, per dozen 1 80

*ONE-TWO, BUCKLE MY SHOE.* Illustrated by Courtland Hoppin, and beautifully printed in oil colors. Twelve illustrations. Small quarto. . . . . . . Price, per dozen 3 00

*ILLUMINATED A B C SERIES.* Elegantly colored, with brilliantly illuminated covers, and consisting of—

    *Pretty A B C.*                 *Fairy A B C.*
              *Child's A B C.*
                                          Price, per dozen 3 00

*NEW NURSERY RHYMES.* Printed in oil colors, on tinted paper, and illustrated by the best artists. Assorted in dozens, containing—

    *Aunt Mary's Nursery Rhymes.*
       *Aunt Kitty's Nursery Rhymes.*
          *Aunt Jenny's Nursery Rhymes.*
                                      Price, per dozen 1 80

*STORIES FROM THE SCRIPTURES.* Printed in oil colors, on tinted paper, and beautifully illustrated. In dozens, as follows:
*The Story of Samson.*   *The Story of Ruth.*
*The Story of David.*

Price, per dozen $1 80

*LITTLE LESSONS FOR LITTLE FOLKS.* Printed in oil colors on tinted paper. Three kinds, assorted in dozens.

Price, per dozen 1 00

*CHILD'S BIBLE STORY BOOKS.* Printed in oil colors, on tinted paper. Three kinds, assorted in dozens.

Price, per dozen 1 00

*A SET OF CHINA.* A charming series of Chinese Story Books, printed in brilliant oil colors. With original designs by H. L. Stephens. The series consists of—
*Fun and Hey-Ho.*   *So-Sli and Ho-Fi.*
*Fum-Fum and Fee-Fee.*
Assorted together. . . . . . Price, per dozen 3 00

*THE ILLUMINATED BOOK OF NURSERY RHYMES.* Printed in oil colors, on tinted paper. Containing nearly one hundred illustrations, and bound in boards, with illuminated cover. Quarto.

Price, in boards per vol. 75

---

*TALES OF OLD ENGLISH LIFE; or, PICTURES OF THE PERIODS.* By William Francis Collin, LL.D. Author of "History of England," etc. In crown 8vo, toned paper, cloth extra, full gilt . . . . . . . . . . . 2 25

*THE IMPROVEMENT OF THE MIND.* By Isaac Watts. An entirely new edition, carefully revised, uniform with the above in style and price . . . . . . . . . . 2 25

# POETRY.

Beautiful editions, elegantly printed and bound, and illustrated with fine steel engravings, for gifts, the drawing-room, the boudoir, and the Library.

*⁎* The Publisher begs to call the Special Attention of the Trade to these new editions of the Favorite Standard Poets, embracing some fourteen entirely different styles, from the smallest readable "Brilliant" to the "Royal Octavo Antique," making the most perfect assortment ever offered in the United States. They are printed on superfine paper, and bound by Somerville in his best manner.

*THE "BRILLIANT" EDITION OF THE POETS.* Elegantly printed on toned and laid paper, and handsomely bound in extra cloth, gilt tops. 24 volumes now ready, forming a very complete library of Poetry. Good legible type, and the smallest and most portable editions of the Poets ever published, and at the extraordinary low price of 56 cents per volume.

| | | |
|---|---|---|
| *Cowper.* | *Lady of the Lake.* | *Wordsworth.* |
| *Southey.* | *Campbell.* | *Lalla Rookh.* |
| *Montgomery.* | *Poetry of Flowers.* | *Mrs. Norton.* |
| *Scott.* | *Eliza Cook.* | *Coleridge.* |

The above 12 volumes put up in a handsome case. . Per vol. 56

| | |
|---|---|
| *Milton.* | *Thomson and Gray.* |
| *Goldsmith.* | *Mrs. Hemans.* |
| *Poetry of Sentiment.* | *Mary Howitt.* |
| *Pollok's Course of Time.* | *Poetry of the Affection.* |
| *Rogers.* | *Young's Night Thoughts.* |
| *Poetry of the Passions.* | *Mrs. Sigourney.* |

The above 12 volumes put up in a neat case. . . Per vol. 56

*THE LIBRARY OF POETRY.* "Brilliant" edition. Comprising the whole 24 volumes put up in a handsome, substantial, and convenient case. A new and superior style. ˋ · . Per vol. 56

An exceedingly beautiful set of books, and a very useful and valuable present. The 24 volumes for $13 50.

www.ingramcontent.com/pod-product-compliance
Lightning Source LLC
Chambersburg PA
CBHW031849220426
43663CB00006B/554